HOW EVANGELICALS GOT
THE GOSPEL WRONG

Praise for Wolfgang Fernández and How Evangelicals Got the Gospel Wrong: Reflections of a Latino Missionary

As a deeply relational person with a big heart and full of vision, Wolfgang could be a catalyst for countless smaller and larger movements – in the beginning churches, later broader Kingdom Initiatives. As such, his life has been a blessing for countless men, women and families in various continents, systems and social classes. Telling his Life story honestly and openly, including his own brokenness and dark times, he shows what God can do through one man – not perfect but faithful.

Reinhold Scharnowski M. Th
Steffisburg, Switzerland

Conflict for a married couple isn't uncommon. Sometimes, all the couple needs is a third voice. That third voice can bring clarity as well as help the couple to hear each other. Wolfgang Fernández, who is considered a citizen of the world, does this for anyone who wants or needs cross-cultural clarity. He also provides real life examples of how to live out a Christ-like model of the Gospel. This book, How Evangelicals Got the Gospel Wrong: Recollections of a Latino missionary is a gift to Christ followers desiring to imitate Christ in community. It isn't an attack on conservative evangelicals, but a revelation. This book is a goldmine. Digging for gold can be challenging, but well worth the effort! Wolfgang has strategically place gold nuggets for us to unearth as we read. If you desire to unify Christ's body, then, this book is a MUST read!

Dr. Clarence Shuler, President/CEO
BLR: Building Lasting Relationships

Wolfgang Fernández's well-storied life leaps off the page like scenes from an adventure film, yet his memoir unveils a deeper story than dazzling tales alone. Behind rich scenes widespread, his vulnerable authenticity charts profound personal growth amid life's rough and smooth. Despite society's inward bent, he boldly bares all—the good and the bad—as one hungering for God rather than reputation. Where institutionally-instilled constraints may have isolated another, his sojourn from mainstream evangelicalism's center to its margins brought greater community, gratitude, and generosity instead. Ever the humble learner rather than resenter, he gifts readers the hard-won fruits of a life-long quest to follow God wherever it may lead. For me, having long admired his staying power against isolates, I'm inspired by this timely reminder: the Kingdom that changes everything dwells within reach of us all. Let us join the adventure!

Shannon Hopkins
Advocate for Innovative
Church Foundations

I am personally moved by the authenticity of Wolfgang's sharing of his life through the pages of his book, where he unveils the profound influence of his family and faith on his missional journey. Through the lens of his upbringing, Wolfgang paints a vivid portrait of his mother's unwavering devotion and her Godly impact on his life. This revelation resonates deeply and inspires me, in my role as a mother, to nurture and pray for my children's love for God and humanity.

Wolfgang simplifies the understanding of the gospel of Jesus Christ as loving those around us, and through that, we express our love for God. His reference to Jesus teaching His disciples to pray "Let your Kingdom come on earth as it is in Heaven.", leads us, as Jesus' followers today, to reflect Heaven's values on Earth by mirroring Jesus' love, mercy, and justice. Through stories and reflections, Wolfgang paints a picture of God's love in action, showing how it can touch and change lives when we share it generously in our everyday lives. In essence, I see the Gospel in a tangible way through the transformative power of God's love that is made accessible to the individuals that Wolfgang encounters in his book."

Cheryl Lim-Tan
Singapore

Life is a journey. It is spiritual in nature. It has many 'players' whose entrance and impact in our lives are not within our scope of determination.   But nevertheless, they are part of 'who we are'. Only God is the One who is painting this incredible picture on the canvas of our lives. And every painting is unique, more valuable than any price that could be paid for it, and leaving this earth a better place than before it was painted. Wolfgang Fernandez' spiritual journey of life is all of this. Have a joyful experience watching the painting unfold as Wolfgang lets you see every detail that's been put on the canvas of his life by the hand of God.

Jim Yost
COMMUNITY for
Life Member

When my wife Rocío and I first met Wolfgang and Vivien in 2010, we sensed we were meant to be lifelong friends. Wolf's cultural curiosity and genuine love was as visible as the tattoo of the cross on his wrist. These last 13 years of journeying together have brought with them countless prayer, challenges to the status quo and an appropriate amount of irreverence. One of my favorite lines from this book is: "while the Lord may have chosen me for a particular purpose, He has equally chosen countless others." Wolf profoundly demonstrates this effortlessly, almost as a reflex. I've been lucky enough to be in the room multiple times when a person much younger than him presents him with a new thought...one that's obviously been inspired by the Holy Spirit. Without missing a beat Wolf will ask this younger person to mentor him in this way of thinking. What humility! My life has been profoundly affected by his outlook on life, and if you spend some time with his words in this book, yours is likely to be as well.

Matt Elsberry
Co-Chief Executive
Officer LivFul

In 'How Evangelicals Got the Gospel Wrong,' Wolfgang takes readers on a profound journey of faith, tracing his life across 70 countries and reflecting on transformative relationships that shaped his understanding. With poignant insight and personal anecdotes, Wolfgang explores the core teachings of Christianity and laments the misconstrued essence of the Gospel in modern Evangelicalism. He delves into history, highlighting a crucial shift from a message of love and community to one marred by political expediency and exclusion. Through vivid narratives from his 45-year missionary journey, Wolfgang illuminates redemptive models and societal barriers, sharing his own struggles and revelations. With serious concern and a warning tone, he challenges the prevailing narrative, offering optimism for a resurgence of inclusive, love-rooted church movements. 'How Evangelicals Got the Gospel Wrong' is a compelling call to reexamine and reclaim the foundational message of Christianity." Wolfgang's perspectives have a profound impact on my personal understanding of the Kingdom of God, that led to my journey in seeking new expressions of it."

Yau Boon Lim
Singapore

HOW EVANGELICALS GOT THE GOSPEL WRONG

REFLECTIONS OF A LATINO MISSIONARY

by
Wolfgang Fernández

For Information, Contact:

Distributed by Skinny Brown Dog Media

Email: Info@SkinnyBrownDogMedia.com

SkinnyBrownDogMedia.com

How Evangelicals Got the Gospel Wrong

Reflections of a Latino Missionary

Wolfgang Fernández

Library of Congress Cataloging-in-Publication Data

ISBN 978-1-957506-79-1 (trade paperback)

ISBN 978-1-957506-80-7 (eBook)

ISBN 978-1-957506-78-4 (hardcover)

ISBN 978-1-957506-81-4 (case laminate)

DEDICATION

To Vivien 蔡慧雯 one who came from the East and together walks hand in hand the second half of our lives.

A WORD OF THANKS

I am deeply grateful to my eldest daughter, Danilee Skye. Not only did she dedicated time to review and correct this manuscript, but she also ensured the accuracy of our family's events mentioned. Her positive reflections on my writings have been invaluable.

Dave Nothhelfer, an adopted member of our family, played an instrumental role in the creation of this memoir. He once shared, "The Lord impressed on me that you must write your story." Dave's encouragement and accountability have been a driving force. Thank you, Dave.

My younger brother, Carlos Wilfredo, despite not being an avid reader, has authored three books, filled with divine-inspired poetry. He shared writing strategies with me and ensured I stayed on course.

A myriad of friends worldwide have opened their homes and hearts, enriching my life with diverse perspectives. A special mention goes to Olav and Unni Råmunddal of Nesodden, Norway, who have been parental figures to me for many years.

To everyone featured in this narrative, you've enriched my life with glimpses of Christ's essence. I'm reminded of the words by Thomas à Kempis from "The Imitation of Christ" penned on August 8, 1471, "We must imitate Christ's life and his ways if we are to be truly enlightened and set free from the darkness of our own hearts."

CONTENTS

ACKNOWLEDGEMENTS

Reflecting on the past 50 years of my life journey, a profound insight by Søren Kierkegaard (1813-1855) Danish theologian and philosopher resonates with me. It's often paraphrased as, "Life can only be understood by looking backward; but it must be lived looking forward."

My life has been a rich web of relationships, spanning 70 countries on five continents. The foundation of this key element was laid by my dedicated mother, Raquel, a visionary woman who infused my early years with unwavering love and determination. My father, Daniel, imparted to me his deep, unwavering faith. He was my spiritual compass, guiding and nurturing my growth until his untimely departure at the age of 53. Their combined influence created a strong and nurturing soil where the roots of my character and faith could grow.

An early lesson I cherished is the realization that life flourishes when embraced with open hands. The more tightly we cling to something, the greater the risk of it slipping away. I practice this philosophy to my relationships with my eight children, each one with her or his personality, strengths and weaknesses; each one brining their unique perspective, love and care enriching my life. Over the years, I matured as a father, actively seeking their perspectives and experiences. This shared experienced deepened our bonds, turning parent-child relationships into lifelong friendships.

The vast web of relationships that have woven through my life served as signposts. Each relationship illuminated my path, providing guidance, lessons, and cherished memories. My Venezuelan heritage played a pivotal role, gifting me with a relational ethos that naturally drew me towards individuals who had wisdom to share. This memoir offers a window into some of these transformative relationships.

Elena, my beloved Abuelita, had a special way of grounding me in faith. She frequently recited Psalms 23 and 91, ensuring I memorized them during my formative years. Those verses served as pillars during challenging times, offering solace and direction. Both she and my Abuelito, Rosendo, instilled a deep-seated knowledge of God that has been instrumental in shaping my worldview.

My identity has been sculpted by every grace-filled moment I've encountered. I find the divine in every aspect of life - in every breath, step, sight, and sound. It's a constant reminder of the Creator's touch, evident in the broken fragments and the beautifully restored pieces of life.

"Let your Kingdom come on earth as it is in Heaven."
Gospel of Matthew 6:10

FOREWORD

Meeting Wolfgang Fernandez in a hotel elevator in Sheffield, England was one of those moments in my life where my world would never be the same. It was the year 2000AD and I had moved my family from USA to the UK only a month before. The occasion was an international gathering that Wolfgang had organized for young leaders who were starting churches and ministries for a new generation in Africa, Asia, Latin America, North America and Europe. Wolfgang and I were both global networkers but working on different continents. Over the next few years, we partnered together to create gathering events all over the world. These events register in my mind as some of the most important things I have ever done.

Now, more than two decades later, our worlds are still intertwined, and we have both matured in age and, I hope, wisdom. The ministries to which we now give our attention are also different than they were . . . more holistic, leading to a much wider range of transformational impact, with a greater level of financial sustainability, and measured by a more accurate set of metrics.

Just as we have changed, so the world has changed and the church's missional response to it. And this is why I feel Wolfgang's writings are so important. Over his past 40+ years in ministry, he has widened and deepened the extent of his missional impact from a very shallow numbers-focused church planting movement popular in the 1980's and 1990's to a rich portfolio of missional social enterprises that encompass agriculture, micro-business, health, addiction recovery, racial reconciliation, job training for ex-prostitutes, holistic Seminary training and forming Jesus-centered communities in and around these exciting clusters of Kingdom activity.

Not only has Wolfgang done these things, but he has done these things years before other missionaries in his field have even thought of them, giving the trajectory of his life and mission a sharp, prophetic edge. Wolfgang has consistently been ahead of the curve, often one of the first leaders at the onset of new movements within Christian missions and occasionally, one of the first to leave when those movements either grew stale or lost their way. Wherever the world of Christian missions is headed, Wolfgang has already been.

In both introducing and recommending this book, I need to say that Wolfgang's style of writing is not dynamic. It is not punchy. It lacks superlatives and exclamation points. There are no catchy memes or one-liners that will ever become bumper stickers. Rather, it reads exactly like Wolfgang talks . . . soft-spoken, humble, relational, unassuming and yet deeply impactful. But mostly, it is relational, thus the elevated place of friendships and the ways in which we can influence each other and spur each other on to love and good deeds. (Hebrews 10:24).

The world of Christian missions is rapidly changing, and it needs to change even faster. In this book, Wolfgang Fernandez not only talks about those changes, but he models them and shows us by example how they will play out. Enjoy!!!!

Andrew Jones
Founder, The Boaz Project.
Tallskinnykiwi.com

INTRODUCTION

The word "Gospel" derives from the Greek term euangelion, meaning "good news." The initial four books of the Christian Bible employ euangelion to describe the revelation that Jesus ushered in God's reign through his life, death, and resurrection.

In the Gospel of Matthew 28:18-20, Jesus provides his disciples with explicit instructions: "All authority in heaven and on earth has been given to me. Go therefore and make disciples of all nations, baptizing them in the name of the Father, Son, and Holy Spirit, teaching them to obey everything I have commanded you."

Jesus highlights the importance of love in Matthew 22:37-40, emphasizing the two paramount commandments: love God wholeheartedly and love your neighbor as you do yourself. Loving oneself is intuitive, as evidenced by my routine of caring for my basic needs. Similarly, loving one's neighbor, whether it's Ray from across the street or individuals from distant lands, emanates from understanding their intrinsic needs.

By loving those around us, we express our love for God. This profound message is the essence of the Gospel. Yet, how did many Evangelicals in the United States misconstrue this?

Tracing back to Jesus's earliest followers, we find they established communities based on mutual support, challenging existing power structures. However, with Emperor Constantine's conversion in 300 AD, Christianity shifted from being persecuted to popular, prioritizing hierarchical structures over the core message of love. Over time, the essence of the Gospel was diluted.

Fast forward to the modern United States, where the Gospel's message is often overshadowed by intolerance and ignorance. A significant portion of white evangelicals supported right-wing ideologies, echoing sentiments of a Christian, predominantly white America. This support was driven by political expedience and moral battles, evident in their stance on topics like abortion and LGBTQ rights.

The country's moral compass shifted as it became more diverse. Historically, white Christian culture dominated, but societal challenges emerged, from drug abuse to the AIDS epidemic, and the Christian community reacted by fortifying its boundaries, notably with movements like Home Schooling. This movement, though helpful in some respects, often portrayed a skewed version of American history, sidelining grave injustices.

While Evangelicals were deeply engaged in these moral battles, their numbers were taking a hit. People voted with their feet turning Sunday, the once considered holy day of the week into a time of personal leisure. Through the 1990s and by 2017 PRRI (Public Religion Research Institute) released data showing how the American religious landscape was undergoing a dramatic transformation. White Christians in the US had been reduced to only 43% of the population. Most alarming was the fact that these numbers represent an aging community. Only 11% of white evangelical Protestants, 11% of white Catholics and 14% of mainline protestants were under the age of 30.

Predictably, these numbers have continued to decline. The current fastest growing "religious" group in the country are those with no religious identity, often referred as "nones" because of how they answer the question "what is your religious tradition?". They can't find any sense of belonging in churches that have become politized towards so called "conservative" causes.

In this memoir, I want to delve into the question of how Evangelicals in America might have misunderstood the Gospel, even though it seems so straightforward. I'll draw from my own 45-year missionary journey, sharing personal stories that highlight how I witnessed the Gospel's effects in various nations. Along the way, I've encountered redemptive models that bring hope to people in the here and now, as well as repressive models that hold them back.

I will also share about my own life and how I came close to pushing my loved ones away from Jesus and my journey towards self-awareness. Despite societal upheavals, I remain optimistic. Americans are resilient and creative, but the church's shift towards exclusivity deters many. However, I believe that new church movements, rooted in love and community, are emerging and restoring the essence of the Gospel locally and globally.

FOUNDATIONAL YEARS

THE CONTEXT

Over the recent three years, our global community has faced remarkable challenges. The advent of COVID-19 and the subsequent travel restrictions have reshaped the way we view and interact with the world. This devastating pandemic took more than six million lives, affecting every corner of the planet. COVID-19 disrupted economies, education, and daily routines, changing life as we knew it.

Since I was a young man of 22, I've been on the move, living a life characterized by exploration and immersion in various cultures. My travels took me to diverse countries, from the rich histories of Guatemala and the scenic canals of The Netherlands to the bustling streets of China. This nomadic existence, which spanned a spectacular four decades, was suddenly put on hold by the pandemic. Each nation had its individual response, and as they implemented lockdowns, curfews, and quarantines, the evening news painted a grim picture of the virus's far-reaching consequences.

Yet, the pandemic wasn't the only event that shook me to my core. The images of the U.S. Capitol, a long-standing symbol of democracy and freedom, under siege by American citizens during the certification of Joe Biden's presidential election win, were deeply unsettling. All of this hit hard as my family had made the challenging decision to leave our homeland of Venezuela, escaping political unrest and a corrupt regime, in pursuit of peace and democracy in the United States. Witnessing the very institution, we revered as a symbol of freedom and justice being threatened was a stark reminder that democracy is fragile.

Another heart-wrenching moment was seeing Russian forces enter Ukraine. The scenes were reminiscent of World War II's darkest days. My heart went out to the innocent Ukrainian citizens caught in the crossfire — the children, the elderly, and especially those vulnerable ones in orphanages, many of whom had physical or mental disabilities. Their plight and the sheer scale of human suffering seemed so overwhelming.

From the safety of my home in sunny California, these global upheavals felt surreal. The world I had traveled and loved seemed to be unraveling.

A disturbing commonality among these crises was the way some participants invoked the name of God as justification. Such proclamations of "Gods will" were used to enforce their views on others, demanding blind allegiance and threatening dire consequences for non-compliance.

During this time of isolation and reflection, I delved deeper into my beliefs and experiences. One memory that often resurfaced was of my early days in a U.S. church. The Cross, which stood tall in the sanctuary, symbolized the love and sacrifice of Christ. Yet, its significance seemed to be diluted, standing next to two national flags. One was the U.S. flag, a beacon of hope during my younger years in Venezuela. The other, a "Christian flag," was unfamiliar and its presence in a place of worship raised questions.

To me, the Cross always represented the boundless love of Christ, a love that transcends borders and human-made divisions. The flags, on the other hand, were emblems of territorial and human limitations. This incongruity took me years to articulate, but once recognized, it became a pivotal point in my spiritual journey.

As a grandfather, my wish is for future generations to embrace and perpetuate love in its purest form. As a father, I reflect on the lessons and values I've imparted to my children. And as a friend, my interactions with a diverse group, from those battling racial prejudices to professionals adapting to global changes, have been invaluable.

I can't help but reflect on the tapestry of beliefs and experiences that have woven together to create the journey of my life. It's been complex and colorful, filled with twists and turns that I never saw coming. Through the pages of this memoir, I've attempted to untangle the threads, to shine a light on the very core of what Love and Life mean to me. It's been a process of discovery and revelation, and I'm grateful for every moment of it.

VENEZUELA CHILDHOOD YEARS

I was born in Venezuela during the tumultuous overthrow of dictator Perez Jimenez by a group led by Rear Admiral Wolfgang Larrazábal. Like many of my time, I was named Wolfgang in honor of this democratic forerunner. Sadly, many successors failed to uphold Larrazábal's honorable example.

In Venezuela, politics and religion, mainly shaped by the Roman Catholic Church, intertwined deeply. My family, however, was an exception. With both grandfathers being Evangelical pastors, Sundays meant attending Sion Presbyterian Church, a church that had been influenced by American missionaries. This religious background made me realize how different my understanding of God was from my peers, often perceived as party spoilers for avoiding alcohol and tobacco.

Growing up, I often felt different and a bit out of place. My mother, Raquel, having learned English in Trinidad, instilled in me the importance of knowing English from an early age. The American School, founded by U.S. Presbyterian missionaries and attended predominantly by children of U.S. oil executives, provide a great learning environment of both my English language training and understanding of the American culture. This, opportunity combined with my mother's influence, proved to be a great benefit to me on my many journeys to English-speaking regions, like Port of Spain, Trinidad and later in the U.S. These trips outside our community in Venezuela expanded my worldviews, especially the summer I spent in El Paso, a farming town in Illinois. Those days on the farm provided a sense of freedom that offered me time for spiritual introspection and self-discovery.

Back in Venezuela, high school had its challenges, being the only Evangelical in a class of 1,000 could have been very isolating. But instead of feeling isolated, I used this as a bridge of understanding. My unique faith journey, coupled with my fluency in English, allowed me to foster bonds in environments unfamiliar with my beliefs.

My adventurous spirit persisted post-high school. A 45-day European bus tour with my mother was followed by enrollment at a renowned Catholic University. By 18, I'd been to 14 countries, immersing myself in diverse histories and cultures.

Daniel, my father, from whom I received my middle name grew up in modest circumstances. In an unexpected twist, he fell for my mother, a chorizo factory owner's daughter. Their union was a love story that transcended societal boundaries. Although he lacked formal education, my mother's ambitions for him guided his path. He transitioned from jewelry crafting to military intelligence, and finally into politics with Acción Democratica, a center-left party. Observing its rampant corruption, he envisioned an alternate political party, ORA Organización Renovadora Autentica, even aspiring for Venezuela's presidency.

However, life took unexpected turns. My decision to attend Bible College in Toronto disrupted his plans for me. He imagined me earning a law degree, aiding him in reshaping Venezuelan politics. Instead, I felt a calling towards theological education and pastoral service.

LESSONS FROM FAMILY

THE WISDOM OF MY FATHER: FAITH AND POLITICS MEET

In 1976, amidst the US bicentennial and the Montreal Olympics, my father organized a trip for me. Starting in Boston for the 4th of July, it led to Montreal for the Olympics. Thanks to his connections, I got access to the Olympic Village via the Venezuelan delegation. In Montreal, my European French from school was inadequate for the Québécois "Franglais." I found comfort at an English-speaking church, where I met Paul Holmes. Discovering my legal aspirations aligned with my father's political dreams, Paul shared his wish to become a missionary. This left a deep impression on me.

Coming home, I told my dad about my desire to seek God's purpose rather than law school. He swiftly voiced his disapproval, arguing that I hadn't experienced enough hardship. My mother, however, stood by me. During a prayer gathering, Magdalena, an illiterate devout woman, foretold my global calling, mentioning a place she termed "Carada" – mistakenly referring to Canada.

Dad's support was withdrawn. He refused to finance my pursuits unless I continued law. So, I took a job as an international phone operator, connecting global calls. The gulf between my father and me widened.

A chance meeting with Pastor Sam Olson opened doors. Leading Venezuela's largest church and founding Hogar Vida Nueva, our first Evangelical Drug rehab center, he offered me a vital role. I assisted Manuel, a former criminal, and watched him find solace in scriptures. Through his eyes, the Gospels came alive for me.

Working both at the call center and the rehab was demanding, but invigorating. Yet, my father held back, anticipating my return to academics.

An invite to a conference with Rene Padilla, a renowned Ecuadorian theologian, introduced me to the Lausanne Committee for World Evangelization. The concept of "Integral Mission", blending evangelism with social activism, resonated deeply, mirroring Manuel's transformation. The challenge was clear: Why let some hear the Gospel multiple times when others hadn't even once? It was a call to evangelize the unreached.

This conference ignited my drive. My travels in Europe, the US, and Canada showed that I could impact any place. What I didn't foresee was how meeting figures like Jim Montgomery, Ralph Winter, and C. Peter Wagner in Lausanne would significantly influence my journey."

CANADA AND THE LESSONS FROM MY FATHER

After a profound conference experience, Canada became the next stop in my journey, particularly Toronto. Paul Holmes, whom I met in Montreal, had introduced me to Ontario Bible College (now Tyndale University), where he had studied. With excitement and determination, I applied and was accepted after successfully passing the TOEFL.

Although thrilled, I had no idea how I'd finance this adventure. Surprisingly, just before my departure, my mother gifted me a plane ticket to Toronto, with a stop in Mexico City, and a check covering my first year's tuition and living expenses. Thirty years later she disclosed that she had sold her precious jewelry, handcrafted by my father, to support my dreams.

Although my father disapproved, my mother's support bolstered me. However, the journey had its challenges. In Mexico City, I learned an important lesson about faith after almost losing all my belongings to a deceitful taxi driver. This situation reminded me of a tense episode in high school when my brother and I had a run-in with aggressive soldiers. Both experiences deepened my faith.

Upon arriving at Ontario Bible College, I felt a strong sense of purpose. My parents' legacy of respect, love, and honor guided me. My father's humility in his later years shaped my understanding of life, while my mother's leadership, commitment, and grace continue to influence me. They taught me to serve and love unconditionally.

In Canada, I adjusted quickly, forming new friendships. One significant activity was Christian Service, which allowed me to interact with refugees from Pinochet's regime in Chile and other parts of South America. The local indigenous community introduced me to Canadian winter activities, enhancing my appreciation for the country and its people.

During my stay, I observed Canadians' distinct perspective towards their southern neighbor, the U.S. They seemed to have a more community-oriented mindset and a unique allegiance to Queen Elizabeth II. Financially, I supported myself by working on campus and during the summer at a Salvation Army camp.

In my second year, volunteering as a Big Brother gave me an opportunity to meet incoming students, including a spirited young lady from California who became my wife. Together, we eventually moved to California's San Francisco Bay Area, where I completed my studies and started a Spanish-speaking congregation.

In 1979, our school hosted a Missions Conference. Inspired by the speakers, I felt a calling to lifelong missionary work, marking the start of my global outreach journey.

Our family grew, and while working in San Jose, I assisted another group of refugees from Nicaragua and El Salvador. This deepened my conviction that a church's role extends beyond preaching; it involves practical help. This holistic ministry vision was often at odds with some prevailing religious views in the U.S., especially during the rise of the "Moral Majority."

MISSIONARY WORK

A LATINO MISSIONARY TO THE WORLD: GUATEMALA

In 1980, I became a U.S. citizen, a decision accompanied by personal sacrifices. However, I proudly embraced democratic values, recognizing the complexities of intertwining faith and politics. Although intrigued by these tensions, my gaze shifted towards Guatemala.

In the lush landscapes and vibrant communities of 1981 Guatemala, a significant chapter of my life unfolded. At the tender age of 22, I had the extraordinary opportunity to become the youngest missionary affiliated with OC Ministries (One Challenge). This prestigious ministry had its roots in the initiative of Dr. Dick Hillis. In 1923, a young and impassioned Hillis, only two years older than I was when I began, made history as the youngest American missionary for the China Inland Mission in China.

My training was comprehensive and enlightening. It was spearheaded by Bob Waymire, a man of wisdom, and Jim Montgomery, the innovative mind behind the introduction of the DAWN Strategy (Disciple a Whole Nation) in the Philippines. Under their guidance, I gained not only the knowledge but also the spirit of mission work.

Jim Montgomery, with his vast experience and insight, served as a beacon for me until his untimely death in 2006. He was a visionary who championed the concept of Saturation Church Planting. This method was all about fulfilling Jesus's directive in the Gospel of Matthew: "make disciples of all the nations." Montgomery's pioneering efforts in the Philippines manifested that when church-planting initiatives were actively pursued, it invariably led to a surge in the number of followers of Jesus. This success in the Philippines gave rise to the DAWN strategy. At its core, this strategy was all about giving palpable form to Jesus's love and using it as a transformative force, changing individual lives, communities, and even entire nations.

Upon the conclusion of the Philippine mission, Jim saw a new horizon: Guatemala. He envisioned it as the next nation ripe for the implementation of a DAWN project. Given my fluency in Spanish, my rigorous training by Waymire, and my deep-rooted understanding of the strategy, I was considered an ideal candidate to participate.

Fueling our mission was the unwavering support of several churches. Institutions like Redwood Chapel of Castro Valley, CA, Fremont Community Church, Crossroads Bible Church of San Jose, CA, and Saratoga Presbyterian Church became our pillars of strength. Their support wasn't just spiritual; it was also material. For over two decades, they provided the essential funds required to keep our mission alive and thriving.

One of the standout gestures was from Redwood Chapel, which donated a robust Chevy Suburban, facilitating our relocation to Guatemala. After undertaking a monumental 3,000-mile drive, weaving through terrains and crossing borders, we finally made Guatemala our home. It was a reunion of sorts when my wife's parents flew in with our children, Danilee and Matthew. With my family by my side, I dived headfirst into my mission.

My travels took me to every nook and cranny of Guatemala. I interacted with pastors from diverse backgrounds, aiming to understand the state of faith in local communities and the overarching evangelical practices in a country as diverse as Guatemala, home to 17 million people.

Guatemala, with its rich history, had faced its fair share of exploitation and adversity. Its people, resilient and open-hearted, displayed a deep curiosity and openness to profound discussions about life's biggest questions, especially those about life and death. However, as my mission progressed, I felt a nagging sensation. I began to realize that in my evangelical fervor, I sometimes overlooked the broader societal implications of our efforts, particularly on the indigenous communities.

During my tenure, General Efrain Rios Montt governed Guatemala (1982-83). His leadership was marked by strict governance. Despite his polarizing tenure, Montt's regime did show efforts toward promoting indigenous participation in the governance. Justice, though, is multifaceted and complex, especially in a society as layered as Guatemala.

Reflecting on my journey, I often pondered on the teachings of Rene Padilla, who emphasized the Gospel's dual message of forgiveness and societal justice. As missionaries, our perspective was, at times, limited. Our mission in Guatemala had set the wheels in motion, but the path ahead was long.

Before bidding goodbye to Guatemala, I spoke at the Principe de Paz church in Guatemala City. I tried to articulate my mixed feelings about the work we had done. As I poured my heart out, a woman, in impeccable English, voiced what felt like a divine message, "God is closing this door and opening others."

Back in San Jose, CA, the mission continued. We embarked on new projects, always aiming to understand the church's true impact on the community. Every experience, every interaction, further solidified my belief in the comprehensive implications of the Gospel and its transformative power.

DAWN: DISCIPLE A WHOLE NATION MOVEMENT

In 1985, Jim Montgomery established Dawn Ministries (Disciple A Whole Nation) in San Jose, CA. Upon his invitation, Berna Salcedo from Colombia and I, hailing from Venezuela, were honored to be the first members of this groundbreaking organization.

At the time, I was serving as a pastor at the newly formed Cornerstone Bible Church, an offshoot of Crossroads Bible Church. My role centered around mentoring and training leaders from various cultural backgrounds, guiding them in founding new community-centered congregations. Jim, with his extensive expertise in community church planting, provided invaluable support in all my endeavors. However, he then extended an invitation for me to join him and Berna in spearheading Dawn Ministries. After in-depth conversations with my wife, it was clear she had concerns regarding this venture, especially given our obligations to our young family. Furthermore, leaders within our church expressed doubts about Jim's leadership capabilities. In a candid conversation, I shared my reservations with Jim, admitting I felt more inclined to remain with the church. Jim's response was direct: he stressed that I needed to be fully on board with Dawn Ministries or continue my current path. His passion was evident, and by the time I returned home, I was committed to bringing Jim's vision to life.

The mission of Dawn Ministries was clear: empower individuals with the tools they needed to revolutionize their nation with the Gospel. This Gospel was embodied in churches that radiated the kindness, mercy, and love of Jesus. Our primary goal was to facilitate the establishment of community-based churches across denominations, ensuring everyone, regardless of social or economic background, had access to Jesus within the countries we partnered with. Our responsibility was to connect with those who shared this national vision and guide them in realizing it.

Jim staunchly believed that every church should emulate the love, compassion, and justice Jesus stood for, making His message compelling and relatable to everyone. Drawing from his extensive studies of the church in The Philippines and recent insights from Guatemala, he believed nations could be reshaped by individuals living by Jesus's command to love their neighbors wholeheartedly. Our interactions with passionate individuals in nations like El Salvador, Indonesia, Ghana, and India further solidified our conviction that the movement's era had dawned.

LIMITATIONS OF THE DAWN APPROACH

In 1985, with anticipation and a spirit of service, my family and I made a monumental decision. After accepting the call to be a part of Dawn Ministries, we packed our belongings and embarked on a new journey, relocating to the picturesque landscapes of New Zealand. Our decision was motivated by the local Christian leaders who deeply resonated with our mission and vision, compelling us to serve in their land. We settled in the idyllic village of Raumati Beach, a stone's throw away from Wellington, the bustling capital city.

New Zealand, with its rich history, presented a complex challenge for anyone seeking to establish new churches. By the time we arrived in 1985, the country was considered a post-Christian nation, with less than 30% of its citizens identifying with the faith and under 10% attending worship services. This posed a critical question: In a nation so deeply rooted in Christian tradition, what role did new churches have to play?

My diligent research and ground interactions brought forth surprising insights. Societal dynamics were shifting, and there was an emerging need for churches that could cater to the contemporary concerns of believers. More intriguingly, while many New Zealanders proudly identified as Christians, there seemed to be a general reluctance to evangelize or promote their faith to others.

New Zealand, on the surface, is the epitome of tranquility, with its green meadows and serene beaches. Its populace seemed content, with minimal emphasis on profound existential dilemmas like salvation or redemption. Yet, delving deeper, I discovered layers of cultural narratives. The experiences and histories of the Māori, the proud indigenous inhabitants of New Zealand, resonated with struggles faced by many indigenous communities worldwide, reminding me of issues I had witnessed firsthand in Venezuela. Stories of betrayed agreements between European settlers and the Māori stirred memories of the painful tales of colonization that plague many indigenous narratives. Yet, hope was not lost; the 1970s marked a period of renaissance for the Māori. The era witnessed a rejuvenated emphasis on preserving their unique identity, culture, and traditions, as well as fostering dialogue and reconciliation with European settlers.

As both cultures intertwined, New Zealand's spiritual landscape became a vibrant mosaic. The amalgamation of European Christianity with Māori spirituality birthed unique worship practices infused with indigenous traditions.

A milestone in our journey was our association with Dr. Bob Hall, a distinguished sociologist lecturer from the University of Canterbury. After attending one of my lectures, Bob, recognizing the significance of our mission, embarked on a comprehensive study, supported by DAWN. His research sought to unravel the complexities of societal structures and their influence on church attendance patterns. His insights provided DAWN New Zealand with invaluable data, further strengthening our mission and helping us refine our strategies.

Leaving New Zealand was bittersweet. As a parting token, I was gifted a jar of Vegemite, an acquired taste for many, humorously termed "New Zealand chocolate" by my eldest daughter, Danilee. She found amusement in introducing this local delicacy to her unsuspecting friends.

My tenure in New Zealand was an enlightening experience. It accentuated the nuanced challenges of church establishment in regions with profound Christian legacies. Throughout my life, a strong maternal influence instilled in me a profound respect for women and their capabilities in leadership roles. In New Zealand, this belief was only reinforced, especially recently witnessing dynamic leaders like Prime Minister Jacinda Ardern taking center stage.

Yet, my advocacy for inclusivity in leadership faced resistance within Dawn Ministries. The board, predominantly older, white evangelicals, appeared reticent to diversify. My persistent efforts to champion inclusivity were met with skepticism, reflecting larger ecclesiastical biases that often-sidelined women. The inclusivity that Jesus modeled with women was lost to the preferred patriarchy defended by Evangelical leaders betraying the position the Gospel opened for them.

Jeff Fountain, a renowned figure in Europe's Youth With A Mission (YWAM), once shared a pearl of wisdom that stayed with me. To truly comprehend the challenges of church planting in Europe, he believed one must immerse themselves in European daily life. With a heart full of resolve, I accepted his challenge, initiating plans to shift my family's base to Europe, hoping to further the reach of DAWN.

July 1989 was earmarked for the illustrious Lausanne Congress in Manila. This event promised a gathering of Christian leaders spanning 173 countries. The Philippines held special significance for us; it was the birthplace of DAWN's strategy. During the congress, we collaborated with local leaders, sharing stories and strategies, emphasizing the transformative power of the DAWN vision.

This congress was a golden opportunity for Dawn Ministries to present its strategies and successes on a global stage. In preparation, Jim Montgomery authored "DAWN 2000: 7 Million Churches to Go," a seminal work that chronicled his journey.

And the DAWN movement in the Philippines. Our workshops, based on Jim's insights, were a resounding success. Participants, representing a global audience, left the congress inspired, armed with strategies and a clear vision for the future of the church. Invitations pour in from all continents requesting assistance seeking to understand the implications DAWN had for their countries.

EUROPEAN ENDEAVORS

EUROPE THE NETHERLANDS, GERMANY, AND ENGLAND.

Europe, with its distinct history and cultural diversity, became the next frontier for the DAWN movement. The Netherlands, Germany, and England stood out as prime locations to expand our reach and establish a stronger presence.

My encounters with Jeff Fountain became instrumental in navigating this new chapter. With his roots in New Zealand, Jeff had an inherent understanding of the DAWN movement's principles. Now, as a resident of the Netherlands, he provided invaluable insights into the European spiritual landscape. The significance of his guidance was underscored on November 9, 1989, when the Berlin Wall fell. This event was not just a historical milestone; it signaled a sea of change across Europe. Borders opened, ideologies shifted, and in this newly harmonizing continent, the scope for our mission expanded exponentially.

Settling in Epe, a picturesque village in the Netherlands, marked a transformative phase for my family. We embraced our new surroundings with an insatiable curiosity. Our home in Pasadena became a cherished memory as we nestled into the heart of the YWAM Heidebeek community. Our kids, resilient and adaptable, effortlessly blended into Dutch culture. They became familiar figures cycling around the village, their laughter echoing in the winding alleys, and their tongues soon fluently rolling out Dutch words.

It wasn't just our personal lives that thrived; professionally, too, the Netherlands proved to be fertile ground. The intricate web of railways became my bridge to various meetings, connecting me to influencers and decision-makers across Europe. It was heartwarming to see familiar faces from Manila, now in European settings, eagerly engaging with the DAWN vision. This blossoming of connections was punctuated by Jeff Fountain's continued contributions.

Through him, doors opened to influential platforms like the European Evangelical Alliance, deepening our reach and solidifying our presence.

Our endeavors in Europe had deep-seated roots. Rewinding to 1987, a pivotal interaction set the course for our future work in this continent. Werner Sidler, an esteemed Swiss missionary, chanced upon Jim Montgomery at the Fuller School of World Missions. Intrigued by the DAWN philosophy, Werner envisioned introducing this movement to Switzerland, a country steeped in Christian heritage. When Werner's initial plans encountered unforeseen challenges, the baton was passed to me. Standing before Swiss church leaders, whose lineage of faith dated back to very early Christian times in the continent, was both an honor and a daunting task. However, the reception was heartwarming. Their eagerness and receptivity to our vision signaled a promising future for DAWN in Switzerland.

Among the sea of enthusiastic faces, one stood out—Reinhold Scharnowski, a pastor from Steffisburg. His passion and commitment were evident, and Donna, with her keen intuition, recognized this. She whispered to me that Reinhold could be the chosen one to spearhead DAWN project in Switzerland. Her foresight proved accurate. Not only did Reinhold take the reins of DAWN in Switzerland, but he also emerged as a pivotal figure in DAWN Europa, an organization crafted by European visionaries to encapsulate and expand the essence of our work.

The European chapter of our journey was marked by collaborative efforts, cultural assimilation, and a fervent desire to usher in a new era for the church, one that was both rooted in tradition and open to modern interpretations. Europe, with its confluence of ancient history and contemporary ethos, became the ideal backdrop for DAWN's evolving narrative.

NORWAY

Norway, a nation known for its breathtaking fjords and resilient spirit, became a welcoming haven for the DAWN movement. In this scenic backdrop, Olav Råmunddal, an accomplished architect from Oslo, whom I had had the privilege of meeting back in 1988, and his gracious wife, Unni, played pivotal roles. Their hospitality and deep-rooted faith were palpable. They were the bridges that connected me to Norway's spiritual landscape, which soon led to the birth of DAWN Norge.

It's essential to mention the rich heritage of Norway. It's a land where traditions and stories span centuries. Their tales of Vikings, explorers, and deep-seated Christian values resonated deeply with me. Within this context, meeting figures like Sigbjørn Ravnåsen, a distinguished member of the Norwegian parliament, was both an honor and an educational experience. Sigbjørn, along with his wife Signe, had co-founded the Hauge Institute, a testament to their dedication to intertwining spirituality with contemporary business ideals. Their efforts were a tribute to Hans Nielsen Hauge (1771-1824), who had centuries before, shown Norwegians the path from adversity to prosperity by blending faith with hard work and diligence.

Under the visionary leadership of Øivind Augland, DAWN Norge experienced a transformative journey, metamorphosing into SENDT. This period witnessed the inception of multiple churches that thrived and expanded their congregations. In just fifteen years, from 2005 to 2020, Norway saw the establishment of an impressive 289 new churches. A commendable 63% of these congregations experienced consistent growth, a clear testament to the tireless efforts of leaders like Augland. His influence was so profound that SENDT's reach extended beyond Norway, touching the hearts of communities even into the Baltics.

However, my time in Norway was not solely about professional growth. The personal bonds I forged were equally profound. Olav and Unni, with their unwavering support and deep faith, became beacons in my life. Their guidance and warmth helped me navigate through personal challenges, making them more than colleagues; they became family.

My missionary calling then took me further north to Finland. The serene landscapes and serene lakes provided a calming backdrop as I met with Kari Törmä, a respected figure in the Finnish Christian community. Kari's dedication was evident in his tireless work of building Christian leaders, and his stories left a lasting impression. One tale stood out: the story of Kari and his wife Tertu's marriage. Their journey from discord to reconciliation wasn't just their personal victory but became an inspirational testament to many. Their dedication to not just mend their bond but also help others in similar situations set the stage for DAWN's flourishing roots in Finland.

Yet, amidst the professional engagements, cultural nuances came to the forefront. The Finns, known for their introspection and deep thought, presented a stark contrast to my more expressive Latino temperament. Their responses were often understated, making it essential for me to learn patience and understand the depth behind their silences. This learning curve, at times, felt steep, but the Finnish people, with their genuine warmth, made the journey worthwhile.

One of the most memorable cultural immersions was when I was invited to a traditional Finnish sauna. This experience, though initially daunting, turned into a defining moment. The camaraderie built in the steam-filled room, where inhibitions melted away, laid the foundation for a nationwide strategy for DAWN in Finland.

My European sojourn continued in Denmark, a country known for the stories of Hans Christian Andersen and some of the happiest people in Europe. The vision of DAWN found ready acceptance here. Their church culture was distinct, presenting a harmonious blend of age-old traditions and contemporary communities. Hans Eric Friberg of the Apostolic Church became a friend and guide, helping me navigate the complexities of the Danish spiritual landscape. His warmth made Denmark a place that resonated deeply with my heart.

Germany, with its rich history and resilient spirit, presented its own set of challenges and triumphs. Wolfgang Simson became a cornerstone for the DAWN initiative. Facing adversity head-on, he sought to revitalize the German perspective on church and community. His tenacity and vision led to the creation of new pathways in the spiritual domain.

England, often considered the Evangelical epicenter of Europe, welcomed me with its history-laden streets and vibrant church communities. The March for Jesus movement and the Anglican Church showcased the spectrum of faith in the nation. Figures like Roger Forster and Bob and Mary Hopkins became allies in the shared mission of breathing new life into Europe's spiritual landscape. Their combined vision and dedication led to renewed vigor and unity within the Christian leadership in England, ensuring that the torch of faith burned brightly.

SOCIAL IMPACT IN ENGLAND

The streams of change weaving across England were emblematic of the indomitable spirit of humanity and the transformative power of faith. As I traveled through the English countryside, from the picturesque hamlets of Cornwall to the bustling streets of London, each place told its unique tale of spiritual awakening.

Every church, whether an ancient structure with a storied history or a community growing among the poorest had its distinct narrative. But beyond the brick and mortar structures, the real essence of this transformation was in the lives of the people. They were the living testaments to the enduring power of faith and community.

In the coastal communities in the south of the country, known more for its tourist attractions than religious fervor, a small group of students had started a regular gathering to pray. They attracted more and more with their devotion and openness to allow unique expressions of prayer. These gatherings, which began in 1999 with just a handful, soon drew large numbers emerging under Pete and Sammy Greig as 24/7 Prayer; now a global movement in 78 nations and over 22,000 prayer rooms.

On the other end of the spectrum was the city of Sheffield. Historically an industrial heartland, the city had faced its fair share of economic downturns. But amidst this, a beacon of hope emerged. Several abandoned factories were repurposed into community centers. These weren't just places of worship but holistic hubs offering vocational training, counseling, and even medical services to the needy. The ethos was clear – faith wasn't just about personal salvation but also about community upliftment.

The power of stories was palpable everywhere. In London, I met Shannon Hopkins, an American strategist involved in the fashion and church planting world who came not knowing what her specific assignment was. Since then, she has led and influence the formation of fifteen campaigns, projects and organizations focused on solutions for the community. Remarkable among them is The Truth isn't Sexy designed to address the demand side of human trafficking, looking at working with users of paid sexual services and challenging them to change their behavior.

While every town and city in England had its unique spiritual journey, there was a common thread binding them all – the belief in the power of community. It wasn't just about individual enlightenment but about lifting each other up. It was a collective endeavor, a shared journey.

As days turned into weeks and weeks into months, my understanding deepened. England's spiritual transformation wasn't an isolated phenomenon. It reflected a global yearning – a desire to find meaning, purpose, and a sense of belonging in an increasingly fragmented world.

In conclusion, my sojourn through England taught me that spirituality isn't just a personal quest; it's a collective journey. It's about communities coming together, breaking barriers, and forging a path of love, understanding, and unity. It's about recognizing that while faith can be deeply personal, its true potential is realized when it's shared, celebrated, and lived as a community. And England, with its rich history and diverse mix of cultures, was leading the way, showing the world that when faith and community converge, miracles happen.

DAWN EUROPA

The DAWN Europa leadership team was intentionally crafted to realize a dream much larger than any individual – a collective vision for spiritual growth and unity. This talented and diverse team was comprised of Bob and Mary Hopkins brilliant strategists from England; Brian Mills, a passionate prayer leader from England; Reinhold Scharnowski, pastor from Switzerland; the visionary reporter Marc van der Woude from The Netherlands; Jeff Fountain YWAM from The Netherlands; Wolfgang Simson, the prophetic theologian from Germany; and myself. These weren't just colleagues to me; they were family in every sense of the word. Over the years, I had the privilege of visiting each of their homes, getting to know their loved ones, sharing stories over meals, and understanding their life journeys. In return, many of them had visited my residence, gotten to know my family, and experienced the warmth of our shared meals.

For many of the team members, the deep bond and camaraderie we shared felt like uncharted territory. However, as a Latino, this kind of profound connection and relationship-building was something I had grown up with – it was embedded in my cultural DNA. Over time, as our bonds deepened, an epiphany occurred: the true essence of our shared faith in Jesus was this very connection. This understanding made us overlook minor theological differences or nuances that typically divide Christians. Instead, our common love for Jesus and the belief that He was the only hope for Europe formed the strong bond that held us together.

Interestingly, while DAWN Europa blossomed on the principles of mutual respect, understanding, and a community-driven approach, its U.S. counterpart, Dawn Ministries, took a different path. The latter was structured more like a corporate entity, operating vertically, with defined hierarchies and heavily influenced by business-centric values. While such an organizational model might seem impersonal, it had its advantages. This structure resonated with American donors, and their financial backing was crucial for our projects to take root and expand on a global scale. However, the clear dichotomy in our organizational philosophies signaled potential areas of friction.

My roles, straddling responsibilities between the corporate-style Dawn Ministries based in the U.S. and the community-oriented DAWN Europa, became a tightrope walk. As days turned into months and months into years, Europe's embrace grew warmer, making it feel more like my true home. This sentiment was further solidified when our fourth child, Natasha Nicole, was born on German soil. Naming her 'Natasha' was our way of recognizing the pivotal changes taking place in Russia. 'Nicole' was chosen in tribute to her birth on St. Nicholas day, a tradition that has deep roots in European culture.

During my time in Germany, I had the unique opportunity to work closely with spiritual leaders from countries like Belgium, France, Italy, Spain, and Portugal. Each interaction was an eye-opener. I learned that while the core tenets of faith remained consistent, the challenges faced by churches varied significantly across regions. A recurrent theme was the inward-focused approach of many congregations. DAWN's mission was to challenge and change this perspective. We believed that true spiritual growth was not about merely increasing congregation numbers but genuinely reaching out and impacting for good the community.

Countries like Hungary, Romania, Bulgaria, and then then Czechoslovakia (now Czechia), freshly out of the shadows of the Soviet Union, had leaders particularly eager for spiritual guidance. The church leaders here faced the daunting task of reintroducing Jesus's teachings to generations that had lived most, if not all, of their lives under authoritarian regimes. We adopted a three-pronged approach: listen intently, understand deeply, and then craft bespoke strategies that catered to the specific needs of these communities. Unlike the blanket strategies employed by some U.S. missionary groups, our approach was customized, ensuring that it resonated with the unique cultural and spiritual nuances of each region.

MIDDLE EASTERN INSIGHTS

THE ISRAELI ODYSSEY AND BEYOND

Drs. Steff and Ruth Nash's transition from the bustling streets of London to the historically rich confines of Nazareth in Israel was both a personal and spiritual journey. Motivated by a deep-rooted commitment to serving the local communities, he joined the Nazareth Hospital, one of oldest hospitals in the Middle East. The hospital, a source of healing for so many, was where our paths converged, thanks to a mutual commitment to the importance of the local church.

I was honored to accompany Dr. Nash, drawn to this ancient land by a shared mission: to understand, nurture, and expand the roots of the way of Jesus and church planting. The diverse landscapes of Israel, ranging from the sacred aura of Bethlehem and Jerusalem to the modern vibrancy of Tel Aviv, presented a challenging backdrop for our mission. With clarity and purpose, we sought to map the Christian Arabic Churches, the growing Messianic Fellowships, and the enigmatic communities of Russian Jews who had chosen Israel as their new homeland. During this endeavor, we stumbled upon a rather unique group of Muslims, ones who were devout followers of Isa, the name by which Jesus is known in Arabic.

Every piece of data we gathered was a testament to the region's intricate religious diversity. Yet, presenting this comprehensive research to the local religious leaders proved challenging. Met with skepticism rooted in deeply entrenched theological beliefs, we faced an unforeseen roadblock. But, in adversity, often lies opportunity. A glimmer of hope emerged when a group of Russian Jews approached us. Their profound connection with the Pentecostal believers, nurtured during the repressive days of the Soviet regime, opened doors to the establishment of many new fellowships where Russian Jews embraced the teachings of Jesus with open hearts.

The early 1990s witnessed a seismic shift in the global political landscape. The dissolution of the Soviet Union unveiled vast territories of religious fervor and leadership that had been stifled behind the Iron Curtain. Wally Kuskoff, with his unique Russian-Finnish heritage, became an indispensable guide, navigating me through the spiritual intricacies of this newly accessible region. His recounting of stories of brave souls persecuted for their beliefs served as sobering reminders of the resilience of faith.

The formation of the Commonwealth of Independent States (CIS) in 1991 was more than a political milestone. It provided a rare chance for church leaders from the CIS nations to unify, free from the shadows of past oppressions. The birth of a unified movement, "Nations for Christ," was thus realized, echoing the aspirations of countless believers.

In this transformative atmosphere, Dawn Ministries was given a golden opportunity to serve. We were eager to share our vision of planting churches across villages and towns with leaders from these newly liberated nations. It was during this era of change that I formed a bond with Brother Edward from Almaty, Kazakhstan. His transition from a Muslim background to a staunch follower of the teachings of Jesus was awe-inspiring. His unwavering dedication was evident when he voluntarily translated Jim Montgomery's groundbreaking book, "7 Million Churches," for a significant gathering in Riga, Latvia.

However, the journey was not devoid of hurdles. At the Nations for Christ event, a significant miscommunication arose due to a translation error. My swift intervention ensured the accurate message was conveyed, but it came at a personal cost. Pastor Joseph Bondarenko's displeasure was evident, resulting in an unintended chasm between me and some of my Russian peers.

The subsequent journey back to the US was one of reflection and retrospection. Sharing this flight with former Mayor Tom Bradley, a Los Angeles resident, turned into an unexpected bonding experience. Our discussions spanned a range of topics, from the constant evolution of societies to the elements that seem to remain immutable across generations.

On reaching home, another turning point awaited. Jim Montgomery's decision to step down as the President of Dawn Ministries called for my involvement in this transitional phase. This homecoming had an unforeseen silver lining. My son Zachary's diagnosis with a rare medical condition found timely attention in the US, something that might have been delayed in our previous locale.

1997 marked our move to the picturesque Colorado Springs, CO. Known as the Mecca of Evangelical Christianity in the US, this city was a sharp contrast to the European cities my elder children had grown up in. Their initial resistance to this drastic change was palpable. Yet, the warmth of our neighbors, Clarence and Brenda Shuler, made the transition smoother. Learning about Clarence's role as Director for Black Ministries at Focus on the Family added a layer of familiarity to this new beginning.

Finally, after a whirlwind of travels and experiences, I found myself amidst family. As we settled in Colorado Springs, with its serene environment reminiscent of quintessential American suburbia, the promise of a future filled with cherished memories and family moments beckoned.

AMERICAN REFLECTIONS

BACK TO THE USA

As I stepped into the Dawn Ministries office, the buzz of leadership transition talks was palpable. While the formal attire of the office had become my new normal, I couldn't help but reminisce about the more relaxed vibe and tight-knit bond I shared with my DAWN Europa colleagues.

The reins of the leadership transition talks were held by Steve Steele, a Silicon Valley entrepreneur. Speaking the lingo of foundation executives, Steve adeptly presented the figures and facts they desired for grant approvals. Owing to DAWN's impressive track record and Steve's relationship-building skills, we managed to secure substantial funds. Debates arose: should Dawn Ministries function as a results-driven enterprise or a apostolic band ignited by a worldwide vision? Ultimately, the former perspective won. Steve ascended to the CEO position at Dawn Ministries, while I stepped into the Vice President of Ministries role. With the transition sealed, my heart yearned for Europe. Yet, my calling had Asia in store for me. The thought of enduring extensive Pacific flights was intimidating, but the excitement of venturing into new territory was invigorating.

My eldest daughter, Danilee, found her first year back in the US challenging. Leaving her senior year in England, she had to adapt to an American high school. Despite staying devoted to her faith in Jesus, her bond with her faith and her church began showing cracks during our time in England at the Tilehurst Free Church. Balancing my roles as a father and a "church planter," I struggled with how to aid her during this transitional phase. I was tempted to coax her into attending church as a cohesive family - after all, a missionary's family missing from the congregation wasn't a good look. However, prioritizing my role as her dad, I chose to discuss her sentiments about our church community. The insights she provided revealed a trend. The younger generation felt that the church was lacking, prompting them to seek deeper spiritual connections elsewhere. Even with my hesitations, I recognized her need for spiritual freedom.

Soon, she stumbled upon a gathering called "Redeemed" in a gym. Though endorsed by local churches, it wasn't tied to any denomination. Her curiosity piqued, she decided to give it a go. One Sunday, I offered to drop her off and asked if I could join. After an initial look of teenage surprise, she agreed, albeit with two conditions: I'd make a late entry and keep my distance during the event. What I saw in that warehouse was an eye-opener. A flourishing community of youngsters had created a distinctive spiritual space, one grounded in genuine and relatable interpretations of the Gospel. The unity and comprehension they displayed were often amiss in conventional churches. This journey with Danilee took me down memory lane, reminding me of her grandfather, who, two decades earlier, had given the Gospel a contemporary touch.

TRIBAL GENERATION

My daughter's journey and the leadership shift at Dawn Ministries set me on a fresh exploratory trail across continents. My quest was to comprehend how God was reaching the emerging generations. In Sheffield, England, I connected with Mal Calladine, a key leader of Tribal Generation. Their goal was to create a network that bridged denominational divides and connected youth churches and movements in England. In my heart I sensed this was much bigger than any one country. Seeking to understand what was happening led to meet leaders in variety of locations from Cairo to Johannesburg and all the way to Jakarta.

Unlike the DAWN movement in the Philippines, this blossoming youth movement wasn't a replica of an American model. This isn't to say that the USA didn't have emerging youth church movements, but they hadn't yet formed a global nexus.

Interacting with these young minds was invigorating. They provided a fresh lens to rethink how we could adjust church priorities to better cater to the youth. Our discussions were frank, nurturing, and insightful. The youth felt free to voice both the highs and lows of their church experiences. My belief was that if these youngsters could link with their global counterparts, we could paint a clearer picture of the global church culture and evaluate what was needed to ignite movements that would transform their culture.

During our global gathering in Sheffield, the first of its kind we had attendees from 25 countries, including the USA. With the funds I had arranged for this event, I booked lodgings at the local Holiday Inn. Our days started at the historic St. Thomas Crookes Anglican Church.

A chance encounter at the Holiday Inn with a mysterious individual named Andrew Jones, aka Tall Skinny Kiwi, turned into a lifelong friendship, teaching me about my own biases and cultural insensitivities. Andrew Jones became my partner and inspiration in all things Tribal.

After formal introductions at the gathering, I surprised everyone by inviting them to a local pub, ensuring a truly British experience. Amidst the relaxed ambiance, stories poured out, revealing striking similarities across different cultural backdrops. The shared sentiment was the need for a Global Tribal movement, resulting in subsequent regional meetings in cities worldwide.

Looking back on this gathering, 15 years post the inception of Dawn Ministries, I realized my path had deviated from its initial course. My interactions expanded my perspective on the limitations of denominations and how certain structures hampered progress. Traditional leadership often seemed distant from the grassroots needs of church members, regardless of age. My renewed mission was to empower the youth, recognizing their desire for the liberty to learn, even if it involved missteps. I decided to go and give permission to leaders anywhere who were willing to take the risks.

Pioneers like Martin Dreyer and Mirko Sander of Hamburg paved the way with initiatives like the Jesus Freaks movement in 1991. This group spread across Germany, focused on young people at the edges of culture. In its prime, the growth rate of new Jesus Freaks communities in Germany even surpassed those founded by mainstream denominations.

Out of the Global gathering, a team including Karsten Wolf, Germany; Olgálvaro Bastos, Brazil and Andrew Jones, New Zealand and I was invited by Japanese leaders to come and motivate local youth in devising their outreach initiatives. As a result of the impetus created, youth-led churches were strengthened and new ones continued to pop up across Japan, a country the revers tradition. This dynamic group of youngsters dared to challenge the status quo and achieved incredible success.

Olgálvaro Bastos, a Brazilian pastor from the Sal de Terra church in Uberlândia, narrated how budding churches were nurturing diverse youth cultures in Brazil. The youth movement was on the rise, holding annual gatherings. I had the privilege to see this firsthand at their nationwide gathering in Rio de Janeiro. There I felt the community's power and observed their influence on their peers. The assembly was a variety of youth cultures, all ardent followers of Jesus, dedicated to setting up new churches and effecting positive change. Witnessing these youngsters put aside their differences and work cohesively towards a mutual goal was genuinely inspiring.

In Chile, I met Fernando and his disciples, known by local media as Rockers for Jesus. Their church, the Community of the Rejected and Despised, might sound off-putting to many, but it echoed Jesus' message of inclusivity. Their church sessions were characterized by intense headbangers, attracting metal music aficionados, all worshiping Jesus.

In Mexico's heartland, I connected with Daniel Hernandez from Aguascalientes, who built a community dedicated to aiding homeless children by offering educational avenues. Through his endeavors with these children, he and his team unearthed opportunities to activate their faith, infusing fresh vitality into the community.

Back in Europe, during the third Norwegian DAWN Congress, the mood was somber. Church leaders convened to evaluate their church planting efforts, only to be met with disappointing results. Before my talk, I met Stephan Christiansen, a young visionary who introduced me to Jesus Revolution and the waves they were making by preaching the Gospel to high school students across Norway. I decided to invite Stephan to share his insights on the main stage. It was a significant moment, as church leaders observed how youth were changing the game, making strides where they struggled.

Reconnecting with the UK and Ireland, I visited several charismatic churches. What stood out was their shared frustration about their efforts stagnating. While their outreach model had enjoyed early success, the youth couldn't connect with it anymore. It was evident that a revamp was overdue.

Despite hailing from different backgrounds, these youth leaders shared a common thread – they all resonated with the Gospel, offering innovative solutions to reach their peers. I became increasingly convinced that the church needed a fresh perspective, one that was open to change and could bridge the generational gap.

ASIAN EXPERIENCES

WHEN WAVES WHISPER WARNINGS - THE INDONESIA EXPERIENCE

As I set foot in Jakarta, the bustling capital of Indonesia, the distinction of the region was palpable. Here, I was introduced to Samiton Pangella, a charismatic megachurch pastor who led thousands and boasted a fascinating history of converting friends from Buddhist backgrounds to Christianity. His vision for Abba Love Church was unmistakable: train and empower the next generation of leaders, laying the groundwork for what would become known as Tribal Generation. The synchronicities between the Tribal Generation initiatives in England and Indonesia, despite their geographic distance, was a revelation that astonished me.

Samiton's ministry, however, wasn't confined to his church. His outreach extended to the working-class Chinese community. Located in a neighborhood predominantly populated by working-class Muslims, Abba Love was more than just a church. It symbolized unity and community service. The bond between the church and the surrounding community became evident during the unsettling riots following President Suharto's downfall. In a display of unity and gratitude, the local Muslim community encircled the church, safeguarding it from the aggressive rioters who wreaked havoc across Jakarta.

The journey from Colorado Springs to Jakarta was grueling, demanding a 26-hour travel duration, compounded by a loss of an entire day due to the Pacific's date line. Despite the physical strain and jetlag, the purpose and determination fueling my travels kept me resilient. I visited Indonesia over 40 times, amassing a wealth of experiences and insights that reshaped my perspective on spirituality, leadership, and community.

1998 marked my first visit to Jakarta, a tumultuous time embroiled in political unrest and widespread dissent against the enduring rule of Suharto. Allegations of his rampant corruption were rife, with estimates suggesting embezzlements ranging from $15-35 billion. The political volatility culminated in extensive riots, with foreign nationals, including Americans and Canadians, being evacuated en-masse, amidst concerns over their safety. Regardless, I decided to brave the tumultuous environment, accompanied by my son, Michael who was 12 at the time.

My presence in Indonesia during such a critical juncture granted me an unparalleled position. It presented an array of opportunities to advocate for the principles of DAWN and church planting. The essence of my message seemed to resonate deeply with local leaders, creating a fertile ground for the spiritual resurgence I envisioned.

While there, I met Hengki Hartono, a brilliant young leader with an influential role among the youth in Abba Love. As our friendship blossomed, he became my guide, illuminating the nuances of local Chinese culture in Indonesia. Hengki journeyed back with me to Colorado Springs further strengthened our bond, transcending mentorship to feel more familial.

However, nothing could prepare us for the tragedy that befell at the end of 2004. A monstrous earthquake, boasting a magnitude of 9.3, sent shockwaves through Banda Aceh, culminating in a devastating tsunami. Hengki and his wife, Chicha, were in the city during this catastrophe. Witnessing the sheer destruction and loss of life was gut-wrenching. Questions about divine justice and God's plan inundated my mind as I grappled with the overwhelming grief and helplessness.

With Samiton from Jakarta by my side in Colorado Springs, we watched the cataclysmic aftermath unfold on the global stage. An inner calling drove us to aid the victims of this calamity in any capacity possible. Venturing to Banda Aceh post-disaster, the devastation was beyond comprehension. The harrowing sight of debris destroyed homes, and the lingering stench of death confronted me with challenging existential questions. But amidst the despair, glimpses of hope manifested in the form of community resilience, the outpouring of international aid, and the unwavering human spirit.

Confronted by the enormity of the tragedy, I stood by the ocean, reflecting on its dual nature: its tranquil beauty and its overwhelming, destructive power. The same waters that Hengki had once feared had now unleashed an unspeakable horror. Yet, amidst the loss and despair, the resilience of the Indonesian people and their unyielding spirit was a testament to the indomitable power of hope and community.

RESULTS AND RECOVERY

From the data we gathered, we devised a thorough recovery strategy endorsed by the United Nations Development Program. This strategy was tailored to assist the rehabilitation efforts in Banda Aceh. Joining forces with five organizations, our months-long journey set the foundation which led to the construction of six hundred homes, offering new vocational training for survivors, and providing support for those wrestling with psychological trauma.

Parallel to our Banda Aceh operations, we expanded our aid to Nias, a smaller island off Sumatra's west coast. Arriving in Gunungsitoli, Nias's capital, we made our way to the ruined village of Sirombu. An erstwhile 2-hour trip turned into a challenging 8-hour journey due to the wreckage. During this journey, we collaborated with UNDP personnel, who were funded by The Principality of Monaco and UBS Bank of Switzerland for home construction. Despite the challenging environment, and unsettling aftershocks felt during nights in our tents, we pressed on. We even made a detour to visit a newly formed island, an aftermath of the Banda Aceh earthquake. With the support from Monaco, many homes were built. My eyes were filled with tears as keys were handed to including elderly woman who had lost all her family, a testament to hope amidst devastation.

Indonesia, with its many islands, lies atop the seismic "ring of fire." While natural disasters are unfortunately frequent, the resilience and adaptability of its people are unparalleled. A notable figure in this landscape is Jim Yost, a missionary who, along with his wife Joan, answered the call to serve in the tumultuous regions of Indonesia. Despite challenges and language barriers, they dedicated themselves to the service of the local indigenous community. One poignant incident, where a child was miraculously revived after drowning, opened the doors to the hearts of the people leaving an indelible mark on the importance of their mission, deepening their faith and commitment.

Jim and I had previously connected due to shared sponsorship and a mutual interest in youth ministry. His dedication to connecting with the youth, regardless of cultural and linguistic differences, was truly inspiring. His teachings emphasized the importance of understanding and catering to the unique needs of young individuals.

In Bali, he introduced me to Andy Prawira, a former hotel manager whose life took a turn due to drug addiction. His time in prison led him to a profound spiritual awakening, and he subsequently dedicated his life to helping others. Andy's mission was to provide solace and acceptance to the ostracized, particularly those impacted by drug addiction and HIV-AIDS. He, along with Jim, recognized the potential in these individuals and transformed them into agents of positive change.

As Indonesia grappled with religious tensions, Andy initiated the Peace Generation program, conceptualized by Jim Yost. The program aimed to foster unity among young individuals from diverse religious backgrounds. An associate of Andy, Frans Manpopo, took it upon himself to implement and adapt the Peace Generation principles in Bali, emphasizing the need for unity and understanding across religious and cultural divides.

The faithfulness and tenacity of the individuals I met, like Jim, Andy, and Frans, were truly examples to me of servants of Christ committed to the Gospel. Their stories showcased the immense potential for growth, change, and redemption offered by the teachings of Jesus.

Navigating through Indonesia, I was constantly reminded that while adversities are a part of life, our reactions to them shape our identity. The narratives of those I encountered demonstrated that even in the gravest situations, compassion, understanding, and love can prevail. Their journeys illuminated the transformative power of the Gospel, highlighting the potential for positive change. Through these experiences, I've come to believe that, even in the bleakest moments, we can be instruments of positive change, echoing the eternal message of hope that resonates not just across Indonesia but globally.

MUSLIMS IN INDONESIA FOLLOWING JESUS' TEACHINGS

At the heart of Jakarta's bustling AbbaLove Church, Samiton introduced me to Krisnadi, a Sundanese Muslim. He had experienced a profound spiritual connection with Isa, the name for Jesus in the Holy Quran. His aim was unique: he sought to live by Jesus' teachings without converting to Christianity. My immediate thoughts were, "That's a perspective I can understand," and "Let's navigate this path together." Such sentiments strengthened the bond I shared with Kris.

Krisnadi's early life in Jakarta's slums had imbued in him a strong prejudice against Christians and the Chinese community. In his youth, he was indoctrinated into waging Jihad against Christians, leading him to confrontations in Christian-dominated regions. However, an encounter with Isa altered his path, transitioning him from a mindset of animosity to one of love. By the time our paths crossed, Kris had started Father's House, a shared life community. Here, he shared bonds with Jacky, an individual bravely battling AIDS, and Ari, a passionate drummer. The trio, alongside others, gave birth to a Punk band – 'The Believers'. But their Punk spirit wasn't about resentment; the Fat-House band members channeled their rebellious energy into cultivating a community founded on love and Isa's teachings. Their warm reception made me feel akin to a paternal figure, guiding them on Jesus' teachings while absorbing insights from Kris about Indonesia's transformation.

Central to Indonesia's ethos is Pancasila, a philosophy embedded within the nation's constitution and imparted to every student. Youngsters are taught its five pillars, which they recite with pride. Introduced by President Sukarno during pivotal historical moments—namely, the end of Japanese occupation in World War II and the culmination of Dutch colonial rule—Pancasila comprises:

1. Belief in the Almighty God (Ketuhanan yang Maha Esa)

2. Upholding just and civilized humanity (Kemanusiaan yang adil dan beradab)

3. Championing the unity of Indonesia (Persatuan Indonesia)

4. Advocating democracy, steered by collective wisdom and representative deliberation (Kerakyatan yang dipimpin oleh hikmat kebijaksanaan dalam permusyawaratan/perwakilan)

5. Ensuring social justice for all Indonesians (Keadilan sosial bagi seluruh rakyat Indonesia)

However, President Suharto, who succeeded Sukarno and helmed the nation for over three decades, had his own interpretation. While declaring that Pancasila rejected all forms of exploitation, backwardness, conflict, and dominance, be it economic, political, or cultural. His words resonated: "Our version of democracy balances individual and societal interests, ensuring no entity, however powerful, can oppress another. Pancasila, in essence, is our societal and spiritual bedrock." Yet his own administration ruled with an iron fist making the nation subservient to his corrupt ambitions.

My time in Indonesia led me to a realization: the Gospel's perception in the nation was clouded due to its initial introduction via Dutch colonizers, representing not just faith but also foreign dominance. The Gospel, when introduced with the might of the sword, loses its essence. Our task remains to separate its teachings from the vestiges of colonial influence.

Kris opened my eyes to the values of Indonesian Pancasila, which could pave the way for a fairer and more inclusive society. Yet, 53 years post-independence, Indonesia was far from realizing these values. Instead of overcoming Colonialism's vices, President Suharto magnified corruption, amassing an alleged $38 billion in wealth at the nation's expense. Less than

1% of the population hoarded the nation's wealth, leaving the majority in destitution.

Kris believed that the teachings of Jesus held the power to instill the transformative values of Pancasila into Indonesian hearts. Thus, the Father House community began to embody these values.

However Colonial Christianity could not embrace this treasure making Jesus a stranger and a foreigner to the average person.

My time in England introduced me to the rejuvenating essence of Celtic Christianity and the story of St. Patrick, revered for his contributions to Irish culture. Born in England and enslaved in Ireland, Patrick managed to escape, only to return later, driven by a spiritual vision. He utilized Irish cultural beliefs as a gateway to introduce them to the broader truths of Christianity.

Patrick's approach mirrored Apostle Paul's tactics in Athens, who, instead of condemning local beliefs, used them as a foundation to introduce the Gospel. This approach yielded profound results: by the end of Patrick's life, 700 churches stood tall in Ireland, and the nation's influence reached as far as Switzerland. Patrick's teachings resonated in various spheres of life; a transformation documented in Thomas Cahill's "How the Irish Saved Civilization."

Patrick's methods seemed to be the remedy to the colonial mindset. Instead of asserting dominance, he lived among the people, understood their ways, and conveyed his teachings in relatable terms.

The failure of Evangelicals in understanding the true essence of the Gospel presents a renewed chance for rectification. Already, many, like the youth in Indonesia, exemplify Jesus's teachings in impactful and endearing ways.

In Jakarta, I immersed myself in the local culture, forming bonds with Kris and his close-knit group of native Javanese friends. I became acquainted with Shiv, an influential member of Jakarta's Indian community, and fostered my long-standing relationship with Hengky, a Chinese descendant associated with the AbbaLove church. Although these cultures often had clashing beliefs and practices, our small community showcased the Gospel's unifying power. My days oscillated among the industriousness of the Chinese, the hospitality of the Indians, and the warmth of the Javanese.

In the bustling streets of Taiwan, my path once again intersected with Timothy Chang, a pastor I had the privilege of meeting during my work with the DAWN vision in the region. Timothy was no ordinary pastor. With a touch of controversy surrounding him, he left a thriving church ministry to serve in a marginalized community near Taipei. Deeply moved by the belief that true service to the poor entails embracing and living in poverty, Timothy began his mission from a modest apartment, offering refuge to the homeless, the ostracized, and the scorned.

His efforts culminated in the creation of the Hebron Family, reminiscent of the biblical "city of refuge" where those facing persecution could seek shelter and await judgment. I was fortunate enough to live amidst the Hebron Family for extended intervals, and it was a profound experience. The unconditional love, the warmth, the sense of acceptance was palpable. This was a place of transformation, where irrespective of one's past or present, there was always someone in deeper pain, reaching out for your help. Their exemplary efforts in rehabilitation were so outstanding that local judiciary systems started redirecting young lawbreakers to the Hebron Family instead of prison cells.

But their rehabilitation wasn't restricted to just humans. They ventured into 'recycling' objects, with a large thrift store becoming the go-to place for unique finds. They cultivated organic crops on donated land and prepared meals that were both nutritious and affordable. Under the dynamic leadership of Timothy and Monica, along with a dedicated team, they showcased a gospel-centric approach that was holistic, catering to both tangible and spiritual needs. It was a testament to the fact that when the principles of love and gospel intersect, it draws people in, paving the way for a community that heals and restores.

Shifting gears to Hong Kong, I encountered a vibrant group of youngsters, steered by Carmen and Thousand, two students who later united in matrimony. Their ensemble, named YES (Youth Entrepreneurship Services), was a testament to their commitment to Jesus and their vision of instigating societal transformation via righteous and transformative business endeavors. Come 2005, the Hong Kong administration threw its weight behind such endeavors, propelling movements like the Social Enterprise Initiative in collaboration with the Skoll Foundation and, subsequently, the Oxford School of Social Enterprise. It was an enriching experience, crossing paths with those who were honing their business acumen, all while fostering redeeming ventures.

Back in the US, an unexpected call from Jim Montgomery, my former guide and the brain behind Dawn Ministries, greeted me. It had been a while since our last interaction, when he had bestowed words of encouragement upon me during a challenging phase. But this call was different. He shared that he was ousted from his position by the organization's CEO. The subsequent weeks saw us delving deep, attempting to decipher the underlying reasons for the shift in our closely-knit team's dynamics. Our introspection concluded that while fiscal responsibility and goal-oriented strategies were crucial, it was imperative to not lose sight of the essence and spirit of our mission. American tendencies to amalgamate business tactics with mission objectives sometimes cultivated an environment that lost sight of our core values. An ideal approach would involve a balanced amalgamation, prioritizing indigenous leadership and cultivating models that not only drew people in but also nurtured them in the teachings of Jesus.

Power dynamics and leadership roles needed to be fluid and egalitarian. A cyclical leadership model where everyone had their turn at the helm, ensuring every voice was heard and valued, was the need of the hour. Reflecting upon our initial days, I remember suggesting to Jim the necessity of a diversified board, one that echoed voices from various ethnicities, backgrounds, and genders. Despite my insistence, the board remained predominantly monolithic, with a sole addition of a female voice that didn't quite capture the essence of my recommendation. Diversity isn't just about numbers; it's about incorporating a myriad of perspectives to ensure holistic growth and effective decision-making.

CHINA

In 2009, seven years post-divorce, I went to Beijing and wed Vivien. Timothy and Monica Chang, the Taiwanese pastors of Hebron Family, blessed us. Their mission: to support individuals seeking renewal became very personal to us. Vivien's children, Ann, Andrew, and Benjamin attended our modest ceremony.

Life in China was a stark contrast. We lived in the CBD (Central Business District) of Beijing; surrounded by new architectural marvels. The vast airport and extensive ring roads were evident of capital's growth. This city boasted the most luxurious cars alongside street vendors and beggars. A haze often limited visibility, and the scent of charcoal or fuel lingered. Birds were scarcely seen, and urbanization dominated the Chaoyang district.

Adjusting domestically was tricky. Chinese meals were rice centric. To Vivien, my aversion to white rice was bourgeoisie; to me, it was a health choice.

Back in July 1989, I'd tried to smuggle Bibles into China but got caught. This was during China's shift from strict communism to a controlled open market. Earlier that year, the Tiananmen Square incident had happened, a suppressed protest that demanded reforms. The grim past was always on my mind, living close to the incident's site and having to show US passports to attend church, as locals weren't permitted.

Nevertheless, I adapted. I picked up a few words in Mandarin and aimed to make a difference. Beneath the modernization, people sought hope. Interactions revealed an openness to Jesus's teachings.

During Mao's Cultural Revolution, a vast cultural cleansing happened. Yet Tian Tan the Temple of Heaven or more appropriately Altar of Heaven, built between 1406-1420, however, stood untouched. In ancient times, the Emperor, deemed Heaven's son, prayed there for abundant harvests. Chan Kei Thong's "Faith of

Our Fathers" details this ceremony, which showcased the parallels between ancient Chinese beliefs and Jewish Temple worship practices.

Simple queries about Tian Tan's preservation led to profound dialogues. The Cultural Revolution had warped Christianity's perception, but historic sites like Tian Tan spurred introspection.

While Christianity faced brutal suppression under Communist Rule, its followers grew from 3.4 million in 1948 to an estimated 100 million by this time. These believers, however, often remained isolated. Many hoped for a heavenly afterlife rather than embracing their roles on here and now. Yet, biblical teachings emphasize Heaven's descent to Earth (Rev. 21) and the believers' duty to usher it in.

During my research, I discovered a theological perspective among key leaders that seemed to limit the potential of the Christian community. When questioned about their ideal church without constraints, their vision was often centered around traditional elements like large church buildings and choirs, indicating a traditional Western implanted focus on Sunday ceremonies.

These leaders seemed to have a different interpretation of the gospel, drawing more from recent missionary teachings rather than the rich history of their forefathers' relationship with God.

Post Mao-era, especially between the 1990s and 2012, there was a period of relative freedom for Christians in China. The church expanded its reach. But with Xi Jinping's rise to power in 2012, state oppression made a comeback. Numerous church buildings were demolished, and leaders opposing the newly imposed directives were incarcerated.

During my stay in China, I noticed that smuggling Bibles was unnecessary since the Three-Self Churches, sanctioned by the state, already had them. I regularly attended the Beijing International Christian Fellowship (BICF), a large church catering to several thousand members in a theater-like setting, accessible to foreign passport holders. Meanwhile, my wife Vivien preferred the intimacy of local Chinese house churches. As BICF grew, they established new sectors throughout the city. One notable group was "Next," a community of young Christian professionals. Their gatherings, often in spacious restaurant areas, attracted us due to its emerging generation character. We naturally integrated and became a part of their community.

Hospitality was a shared passion for Vivien and me. We loved hosting, providing meals, and fostering a sense of belonging. Recognizing the isolation many felt in the bustling urban environment, we saw an opening to establish a sanctuary. Our residence, strategically located amidst the expatriate community, became a frequent gathering spot. Most visitors, primarily from North America but representing diverse continents, held significant roles working with local Chinese. Our goal was to guide these leaders, equipping them to then guide others in Kingdom ways.

Our gatherings became known for their warmth, with food, drink, and an atmosphere of mutual care. For those seeking deeper spiritual growth, we held dedicated sessions to nurture their faith, fostering a vibrant community centered on spiritual exchange and support.

Building trust led us to further connections. Many were influencing positive societal shifts, valuing individuals for their intrinsic worth. I'd like to highlight three key opportunities that we closely associated with and remain deeply etched in our hearts.

A significant vulnerable group in China consisted of families of the countless workers migrating to fuel the city's rapid construction pace. Known as Migrant Workers, these individuals often left behind their homes seeking opportunities in booming coastal regions. Their living conditions were makeshift and often substandard, used for extended periods. They periodically visited their families during the Chinese New Year but would return to their demanding jobs. As some started relocating their families, challenges arose. The Chinese system provides amenities like housing, healthcare, and education based on one's birthplace, which meant these migrated families often lacked those basic provisions.

Jonathan Hursh, originally from Alabama, USA, started as a passionate entrepreneur acutely aware of the adversities confronted by children of migrant workers. Driven by a sincere wish to create change, he took the significant step of registering "Compassion for Migrant Children" as an NGO in Beijing. Their mission was clear: support these children, who frequently faced inadequate educational opportunities, by offering them a mix of sports, arts, and English lessons. As the days went by, their influence grew and spanned multiple areas, receiving acknowledgment for their efforts in aiding some of society's most fragile members.

Jonathan's belief was that practicing the values inspired by Jesus in Beijing could have a broader societal impact. Their unwavering dedication led to them receiving conditional support from local authorities. Jonathan wasn't alone in this quest. He found allies in Scott, an educator from Canada, and Simon, a legal expert from Australia. Together with other members of the Christian community, they commenced a remarkable journey.

Another vulnerable group the Pakistani community in Beijing. These were mostly Ahmadi Muslims, seeking asylum due to religious persecution back home. Arriving in Beijing after grueling bus journeys with tourist visas, they would approach the UN office for Refugees seeking asylum. While China didn't offer them permanent residence, legitimate asylum seekers had a provisional place in Beijing. However, this didn't come with rights to housing, employment, or health care. Their modest UN stipend mainly went towards rent, forcing them to fend for other needs. Many spent significant time awaiting decisions that might allow them to relocate to countries like the USA, Canada, or parts of Europe.

The collective endeavors of Jonathan, Scott, Simon, and the larger Christian community resulted in genuine bonds with these Pakistani asylum seekers. They shared meals, events, and gatherings, sometimes with groups of 20-30. Such encounters were more than just social; they were bridges of understanding, showcasing that varied beliefs can coexist and even thrive. Relationships matured, leading to some of these individuals visiting our residences and introducing us to their exquisite traditional dishes. Amir, a particularly close acquaintance who addressed my wife as Ma-Vivien, learned household chores, transcending cultural norms. Some even achieved their dreams, relocating to places like Texas and Virginia in the USA. The ties are still alive today, solidified by shared greetings during special occasions like Eid, signaling Ramadan's end.

In this journey, two individuals etched lasting memories: Nai Nai, lovingly referred to as Grandma, and Lao Huang, a handyman whose skills seemed boundless. Nai Nai, a septuagenarian, was a beacon of positivity, always warm and cheerful, even when life threw her curveballs. Her unwavering faith in Jesus was palpable, and she was always eager to spread kindness. She revered her Bible, especially as she once lived without one due to state restrictions. Nai Nai's departure from this world was quiet, but she left behind an ethos emphasizing inner contentment.

Lao Huang's tale is synonymous with numerous migrant workers. Leaving his family for much of the year, he sought opportunities in Beijing, only reuniting during the Chinese New Year. My wife Vivien first met him during one of her House Church visits, and he soon became an irreplaceable asset in her business ventures. His hard work, tenacity, and dedication was evident in every project. His tranquil demeanor, especially in challenging times, stood out. His dedication remains an epitome of true service.

Both Nai Nai and Lao Huang, among many others I've had the fortune to know, represent the embodiment of Jesus' teachings. Their daily lives resonate with the essence of the Gospel, guiding me in understanding the real from the superficial. ·

In the heart of Beijing, our network was enhanced by the influence of local Chinese legal professionals. This web of connections was amplified through Vivien's extensive professional engagements. Among these connections, two individuals stand out vividly in my memory: Bruce and Jane (names changed for discretion). Their insights into Chinese culture and the world of law proved invaluable, but it was a simple dinner that stands out the most.

One evening, we invited Bruce and Jane over to our home for dinner. Amid the chatter, the time came for our 8-year-old son, Ben, to head to bed. When I gently nudged him to do so, he responded immediately. This simple act of obedience astounded our guests. It served as a steppingstone for an enriching discussion about the challenges of parenting in today's accelerated digital world. Interestingly, instead of veering towards a comparison of religious beliefs, our conversation revolved around the core principles of making genuine, life-altering decisions.

Our friendship with Bruce and Jane unlocked doors to other legal minds, curious about the intersection of life, choices, and faith. Bruce, a distinguished Stanford Law graduate, was upfront about his atheistic views. He often steered clear from any religious discourse. However, during one conversation, he expressed genuine surprise when I confessed that my actions sometimes didn't entirely align with my beliefs, reflecting a similar basis to his at atheistic perspectives.

A few years earlier, Vivien and I had the pleasure of meeting Tomáš Sedláček during a trip to Prague. As a celebrated economist and academician, Tomáš was renowned for his advisory role to President Václav Havel. His accolades also included the imminent release of a seminal book The Economics of Good and Evil in China. Intriguingly, despite his deep-rooted religious beliefs, Tomáš found a way to seamlessly integrate faith into his academic endeavors. This holistic approach inspired us to float the idea of a book study group with our lawyer acquaintances. What began as a small collective of a dozen members gradually transformed into a robust platform for deeper connections and spiritual exploration.

Although I couldn't precisely gauge the spiritual trajectory of each member of this group, there's a deep-seated belief within me that we managed to sow invaluable seeds of understanding and friendship. By 2012, the winds of change beckoned us towards the USA, both for Ben's advanced schooling and to be geographically closer to our aging family members. Our departure from Beijing was timely, as it occurred right before Xi Jinping's ascent to the presidency, a period marked by heightened regulations for expatriates.

Our new chapter began in Millbrae, CA. Nestled close to the San Francisco International Airport, Millbrae's charm was in stark contrast to the bustling mega-city vibes of Beijing. Living here came with its unique set of challenges, most notably, the proximity to Vivien's family. On the upside, this relocation was a cultural renaissance for me, as I immersed myself in local traditions and nuances.

Our spiritual journey in the USA began at Menlo Church, a Presbyterian church. Our eclectic experiences from China provided a fresh lens through which we could interpret the dynamic Californian lifestyle. The church's warm community, recognizing the global weight of our contributions, enveloped us in support and camaraderie.

As we retrospectively assessed our years in China, an idea germinated: Why not amalgamate our professional pursuits with our ministry? Vivien's ten-year stint in China's real estate sector, combined with my collaborations with churches worldwide, underscored the significance of living the Gospel authentically, extending its teachings into every societal layer.

Around 2013, my dear friend from Jakarta, Samiton, introduced me to a phenomenal individual, Ibu Sora from Medan. This entrepreneur was on a mission to uplift economically disadvantaged women by helping them kickstart their businesses. Alongside, Sora and her husband were at the helm of a burgeoning church. In 2007, with unwavering support from her spouse, Sora launched an educational institution for the less fortunate, witnessing exponential growth over the years.

Drawing inspiration from Muhammad Yunus's Microloan blueprint, Sora harbored aspirations of initiating a parallel project. In partnership with Pak Subahtiar, a credit union maestro, their vision came to fruition in 2013. The project was uniquely tailored, focusing on empowering women not just financially, but also through a robust support system. Financial backing from a Swiss friend catalyzed the project's expansion.

I was fortunate to observe these businesses first-hand, gaining an intimate understanding of the transformative power of Sora's vision. These regions, traditionally challenging terrains for Christian evangelists, were now accessible due to Sora's sincere endeavors. At the heart of her project was a set of fundamental principles: tithing, diligent saving, prudent expenditure and prompt debt repayment. The ripple effects of this initiative extended far beyond the individual beneficiaries, deeply impacting their families and broader communities.

In comparison to conventional missionary activities, Sora's methodology was a breath of fresh air. Instead of perceiving Muslims as outsiders, she fostered a spirit of inclusivity, finding common ground and mutual respect through shared religious tenets.

In the mix of local communities, it's always heartening to find individuals who passionately wish to uplift their surroundings and make tangible differences in their lives and careers. We saw this transformative potential in Aaron Rau. A chance encounter with Aaron at a mutual friend's barbecue revealed we were neighbors. The zest with which Aaron had bid farewell to his prosperous job at Goldman Sachs, to chase his own dreams, was truly invigorating.

As we started our weekly discussions, our conversations veered towards understanding how the teachings of Jesus could be amalgamated into the corporate world. In these insightful sessions, I got introduced to his colleagues who shared similar inclinations. During this phase, I also met Sonia, Aaron's fiancée, and had the honor of officiating their union. Aaron's entrepreneurial journey was anything but smooth. His initial attempt, a counseling app, unfortunately, didn't gain momentum. However, undeterred, he collaborated with Joshua Reischer, and together they birthed HealthNote – a revolutionary app aimed at simplifying patient registrations for doctor appointments. Their grit and tenacity over the subsequent four years culminated in securing series A funding, marking their spot in a fiercely competitive market.

The association with Aaron underscored an invaluable lesson: businesses built on values of redemption not only can sustain but flourish, delivering value to all stakeholders involved. This indeed is the essence of the Gospel - its real-world relevance that amplifies societal good.

Parallelly, Hogan Bassey and Matt Elsberry's LivFul is a poignant reminder of redemptive businesses. Childhood memories of battling malaria in Nigeria were the seeds of Hogan's dream to eradicate this menace. His academic pursuits in the U.S. led him to devise a formula based on an amino acid that naturally occurs in our bodies– a long-lasting shield against malaria, designed keeping affordability in mind for even those earning merely $3-5 daily. Their chosen company name, 'LivFul', resonates with the Gospel's essence, drawing inspiration from John 10:10. Their roles as co-CEOs are a testament to their shared vision.

Debbie Jones's tragic demise due to malaria left an indelible mark on Matt Elsberry. Debbie, along with her husband Andrew, our partners and close friends since 2000, were a beacon of hope for many in West Africa, mentoring young individuals and instilling in them sustainable farming skills. Their nomadic journey, spanning 35 countries, was dedicated to embracing and uplifting the marginalized, addressing the chasm they felt between church teachings and real-world practices. Before her untimely death, Debbie harbored dreams of educating African women about initiating businesses in sync with their traditions and values, an alternative to mere profit-driven agendas. I remember introducing the Joneses to Matt Elsberry in Indonesia, recognizing the potential of synergies. At that juncture, Matt was spearheading a Kingdom-focused Entrepreneurship initiative in Jakarta, which had garnered significant popularity. Debbie's unfortunate passing stirred a renewed determination in Matt and his wife Rocio, propelling them to join the global crusade against malaria.

These stories really highlight a big change in how we think - putting people before profits. LivFul's approach to making thoughtful products, honoring the natural world, and reaching out to underserved communities is impressive. They believe that embracing values that bring positive change can lead to real solutions, which is kind of like what you hear in the teachings of the Gospel. It's like a path to making things better for everyone – a true road to salvation.

PERSONAL TRIALS
AND TRIUMPHS

MORE WORK, MICROLOANS, AND MEMORIES FROM COLORADO SPRINGS

Back in Colorado Springs, my family and I attended New Life Church, a mammoth church where Pastor Ted Haggard, the influential head of the National Association of Evangelicals, was the mainstay. Being part of this megachurch was a stark contrast to our earlier experiences. Everything was executed on a grand scale – from the hymns to the sermons. Every Sunday, we were amid thousands, creating an ocean of faith.

However, in this vast sea of believers, it was a paradox how isolating it could feel. It was as if being in a crowded room yet feeling alone. With so many attendees, one might think that creating bonds would be easy. However, making meaningful connections was anything but. Most appeared to be in their worlds, seemingly aloof to larger global concerns. Their concerns were more insular, more local.

Every Sunday, the energetic Pastor Ted would bellow, "Are you thrilled to be here today?" Almost robotically, the congregation would roar back with a unanimous "YES!" But for someone like me, who had seen the tumultuous terrains of Indonesia and experienced the pain and suffering there, my heart and soul often whispered a "NO." It was an internal conflict – the disparity between what I felt and what was expected of me. It struck me odd how in such a vast gathering, not one soul ever questioned my subdued response.

The church's decor reflected the local culture. Colorado Springs has a strong military presence, which was evident in the omnipresent American flags. The so-called Christian flag was also a familiar sight. The church was proud of its missionary endeavors. On one special occasion, the church decided to honor its global outreach. I was tasked with guiding two Egyptian brothers from the Middle East. As we walked through the various sections, showcasing our international missions, one display halted our journey. A poster depicted a fair skin Jesus, draped in Israel's flag as if it were a prayer shawl. This portrayal deeply unsettled Sammy, one of the brothers. To him, the Israeli flag was a painful reminder of the military conflicts that had claimed many of his kin. He couldn't fathom how Jesus, the universal Savior, was being used to side with one group over another.

Despite its flaws, New Life Church had immense potential for global impact. Post a prayer session for the Muslim victims of the Serbian invasion of Kosovo, I reached out to Pastor Ted. I suggested we send relief to the refugees in Northern Macedonia. My proposal found resonance, and in the subsequent Sunday service, Pastor Ted made a heartfelt plea to the congregation. The response was overwhelming – both in spirit and in kind. With generous donations, we assembled a team, including medical professionals and engineers, and departed with $25,000 worth of aid.

The church was a perplexing blend of contrasts. From the outside, it appeared unified, but internally, there were underlying currents of conflicts and contradictions. And as time would tell, some of these would become public, shaking the very foundation of this establishment.

Despite my globe-trotting adventures, instances of racism directly affecting me were rare. However, conversations with my neighbor, Clarence Shuler, were enlightening. He shed light on the racial biases that permeated everyday American life, biases that I had been oblivious to. It was disheartening to see the Gospel, which should have been a beacon of hope and equality, turning a blind eye to such a deep-rooted issue.

During one of my town visits, a car sticker caught my eye: "Focus on your own dammed family." It was a pointed comment at the 'Focus on the Family' group, known for their vocal opposition to abortion and gay rights. Why, I pondered, were we getting lost in semantics rather than empathizing with the individuals? Instead of understanding, there was a general tendency to label, judge, and ostracize.

It was disconcerting to see Christianity, a faith built on love and acceptance, being perceived as judgmental. Jesus never mandated a rigid set of lifestyle choices. He merely invited us to walk in His path, a path of understanding and compassion.

In my life's journey, I grappled with these contradictions, aiming to find a balance between faith and humanity.

MY REDEMPTION

From my adolescence, I often felt anxious talking to girls, especially those I found fascinating. A standout memory is of a girl named Tita, whom I met during my freshman year of high school. I was deeply captivated by her innate kindness and her natural beauty without makeup, qualities I still admire in women today. We only ever shared casual greetings; I couldn't bring myself to say more. Over time, I thought this was my own unique issue since my friends didn't seem to struggle this way. I began to view it as a protective blessing, possibly a divine intervention, keeping me away from potential troubles.

Entering college, I discovered a newfound confidence. That's when I met Donna. She had the same natural beauty and kindness that drew me to Tita. Donna became my first girlfriend and the first woman I passionately kissed. Before proposing, I asked if she was ready to travel the world and live in various countries. At 19, I put forth this life-changing question. Donna, at 20, had lived her entire life in the same house. She went to school with the same people from kindergarten to high school graduation, attended the same church, and had a life marked by consistency. On the other hand, I had experienced multiple cultures, traveled across numerous countries, and could communicate in a few languages. Our backgrounds were opposites. Her hesitant "yes" was a testament to our love. After seeking her father's approval over a payphone, we tied the knot the following summer in Castro Valley, CA.

The Redwood Chapel community was made up of sincere believers who were genuinely interested in our union. I recall being asked by a would-be close friend if I was marrying Donna for a green card. Surprisingly, I had no idea what she meant! Despite undergoing premarital counseling and various evaluations, our contrasting backgrounds were never brought up.

Life with me, full of global adventures, was exciting but challenging. For me, overcoming daily hurdles in different countries was thrilling. For Donna, it sometimes resulted in depression. I soon realized the complexities of an intercultural marriage. Donna thrived as a loving mother, focusing on our children's wellness and education.

Years later, when we settled in Colorado Springs, Donna finally felt truly comfortable. Conversely, I was restless in under a year. Being close to my family after two decades brought joy, but it also introduced unforeseen challenges in our relationship.

At my job, I was becoming more involved in Asia, particularly China. I was seeking partners to support this passion when I got an invitation to speak to the Chinese community at New Life Church. My message was well-received, leading to more engagements. I proposed starting small groups to foster a sense of community, but the pastor had a different vision in mind.

That's when I met Vivien Hsu, a recent arrival from Taiwan. She became instrumental in my research about China. We introduced our families and collaborated on understanding the potential of Chinese youth culture and the Gospel.

I've always valued transparency, evidenced by my office with a half-glass door. I've worked with numerous women over the years, always maintaining accountability. Everyone in our office welcomed Vivien.

To grasp her viewpoint, I met her husband. He seemed uninterested in my mission after our second meeting. Instead of taking this as a warning, I became more curious, seeking Vivien's perspective.

A few months later, I had an opportunity to travel to Japan to assist leaders eager to influence the youth culture. Aware that I would encounter many young ladies, I invited my wife to accompany me. When she declined, I extended the invitation to Vivien. She faced a significant challenge due to the longstanding distrust many Chinese held against the Japanese because of the World War II atrocities. To me, this trip represented a chance for healing and reconciliation, reflecting the essence of the Gospel. With her husband's consent and our team's support, Vivien and I traveled to Tokyo.

During our visit, we observed how we each responded to unfamiliar situations and how our individual strengths and weaknesses complemented each other. Our host team, a mix of locals and expats, valued our contribution and expressed their desire for our return. We returned to Colorado Springs with aspirations to strengthen our professional collaboration.

Unbeknownst to me, I was developing an emotional bond with Vivien, and the feelings were mutual. My naturally open demeanor, which many found endearing, became a smokescreen that obscured the budding attraction between us.

Back in the States, a family crisis arose. My eldest daughter, Danilee, revealed she was pregnant. My wife, Donna, demanded she move out, while I believed we should support her. This disagreement escalated, resulting in my heart-wrenching decision to ask Danilee to leave. This event strained my relationship with Donna even further.

I contemplated resigning from my job, thinking that if I couldn't support my daughter, how could I advise other young people? Tensions in our marriage, compounded by our cross-cultural differences and frequent relocations, had created a superficial bond between us. This weak foundation couldn't withstand the tremors of an affair.

My relationship with Vivien escalated from emotional to physical. After hiding our affair for nearly a year, we decided we couldn't continue deceiving everyone. During a counseling retreat I confessed to Donna. Then I confessed to my CEO, who gave me an ultimatum: resign or be fired. After resigning, I faced the painful task of confessing my actions to my colleagues, children, and mother.

Upon revealing my affair, I received meaningful support from my ministry partners. Some even paid for a trip to Indonesia for rest and reflection, while others offered counseling. Although Donna and I attempted reconciliation, she eventually filed for divorce.

Finding solace in my younger brother home, I reflected on my actions and the pain I had caused. My brothers, who ran a successful wood floor business, offered me employment. As I worked, I frequently reflected on the turns my life had taken and mourned the consequences of my actions.

Every weekend, when my kids Natasha and Zak visited, we grappled with the emotional aftermath of my choices.

In the darkest chapters of my life, I found solace in unexpected places. My son Zak, born with a rare genetic disorder, served as a beacon of love. While others might have seen him as someone needing care, for me, he became my protector. His pure joy at our reunions was a balm to my fractured soul. His unique traits were reminiscent of my late father, drawing us closer as a family.

Similarly, my eldest daughter, Danilee, stood by my side when I felt most isolated. When her soldier husband was deployed to Iraq, she and I found solace in each other's company. Our outings and movie nights were more than just spending time together; they were acts of mutual protection.

However, this sense of family warmth was starkly contrasted by the cold reception from the religious communities I was part of. When I left Dawn Ministries, a deafening silence followed. I had hoped for a compassionate approach, one that would acknowledge our collective faults and work towards healing. But that wasn't the case.

Upon leaving New Life Church and sharing my struggles with Pastor Ted Haggard, I was met with little more than a courteous farewell. It pained me to think how often religious institutions choose to sweep issues under the rug rather than confront and heal them. This very act diminishes the faith's credibility, pushing younger generations away from its embrace.

But, as the saying goes, when one door closes, another opens. My salvation came in the form of Vanguard Church and its leader, Pastor Kelly Williams.

There, I was no longer the disgraced minister but a fellow seeker of faith. I was fortunate to find a community that recognized the strength in vulnerability and the authenticity in admitting one's flaws.

Kelly, in his kindness, taught me a vital lesson: true Christianity doesn't thrive on presenting a façade of perfection. Instead, it blossoms when we embrace our brokenness and work towards healing and redemption together.

MY JOURNEY FORWARD

After stepping away from Dawn Ministries, a significant chapter in my life, I took on a new venture with Fashion Hardwood Floors, a booming business owned by my younger siblings. Under Carlos's artistic craftsmanship with wooden floors and Art's dedicated work ethic, the company had built a reputation amongst top-tier contractors, marking its presence in some of Colorado Springs' most elite homes. My income during this period exceeded any of my previous years as a missionary. Yet, wealth was merely a means to pay my bills; the desire for excessive earnings didn't drive me. Sensing this, one day in 2003, a year post my divorce, Carlos and Art came forward with a proposal, "We value your contribution to our business. But we genuinely feel it's time for you to get back to your true calling. We are with you." Their words paved the way for my next chapter.

Their faith in me peeled away layers of self-doubt and guilt. I began to realize that my break was a necessary respite, a time for mental and emotional healing. A fixed timeline couldn't dictate such personal transitions.

During this introspective phase, I met many who shared my experiences and felt that conventional Christian practices failed to provide the needed support. If sin is intrinsically human, what's amiss? The evident truth: we had modified the Gospel to suit our contemporary perspectives. Our focus shifted to maintaining a pristine public facade, meanwhile pointing fingers at others' sins. This mentality resonated with the behavior of Spanish Conquistadors who introduced the cross to indigenous people of America, even as they overpowered them. Similar situations unfolded with my ancestors, the Caribs of the Caribbean, and with many other historical events.

The Cross, originally a Roman symbol of brutal death, transformed its meaning when Jesus was crucified. Through His selfless act, He bridged the gap between the Creator and His creation. His message was revolutionary: "Love one another. As I have loved you, so you must love one another. By this, everyone will know that you are my disciples if you love one another." (John 13:34-35).

Peter, one of Jesus' close followers, was about to disassociate from Jesus due to fear. But Jesus chose this moment to exemplify love and redemption, leading Peter towards self-realization.

The way forward for believers involves acceptance of our flawed nature, coupled with compassion towards others. Such acts of genuine love not only heal us but also attract others towards this accepting community.

Modern churches, however, have drifted from Jesus' teachings, now rooted in power dynamics. The Roman Empire's principle of "Caesar is Lord" got challenged by the early Christians, who boldly declared "Jesus is Lord." This belief saw massive support, with many willing to sacrifice all for it.

However, things shifted when Roman Emperor Constantine embraced Christianity in 300 AD. From persecuted underdogs, Christians suddenly became the power bearers. And with this newfound status, they began wielding the cross and the sword simultaneously, a stark contradiction to their faith. This blend of faith and power was the foundation of Western Civilization, encapsulated in the European legal principle "Cuius regio, eius religio."

Throughout history, rebels rose against such clergy who favored rulers over faith. Their voices, though often silenced, continue to echo.

In my own way, I too defied this system. I experienced profound love and redemption during my lowest days. Listening to my brothers, I moved forward.

Contemplating my journey, I recognized the need for a novel framework to pursue my revitalized mission. Thus, "Next Step" was born. I envisioned this organization to nurture leaders embodying Jesus' values in every life facet. I would share my experiences, both good and bad, to shape their perspectives. I vowed to create a community bound by love, where my past pain would light the path ahead. In 2003, Next Step Ministries was officially established in Colorado.

The positive responses from long-lost friends reaffirmed my path, resonating with Jim Montgomery's parting words, "God is not finished with you yet."

Daniel Hernandez, a former collaborator from Aguascalientes, Mexico, was among the first to join me in this fresh endeavor. Transitioning from promoting DAWN, his heart resonated with the restless youth. Establishing a community hub in his house, it soon bustled with kids, drawn by music, tutoring, and skateboarding. Here, faith met community, emerging as the future ministry model.

My Indonesian friends, excited about Next Step, urged my return. Over 40 trips later, it remains one of the most transformative experiences I've undertaken.

Emulating St. Patrick's approach which transformed Ireland, leading to the establishment of hundreds of churches and influencing Europe. We encouraged youth to embrace their culture and discover within redemptive analogies that could be understood by their contemporaries. We also sought to emulate service to both be relevant to a community and to generate income by establishing solutions to local problems.

I also invested time in Singapore, interacting with Anglican Church members and other community-focused individuals. Among the many good friends, I got to know there, was Yau Boon and his wife Cheryl; he was in a senior position in SAP, the German software company, and Cheryl trained as an architect, was managing Singapore Airlines' development of their exclusive lounges in major hubs around the world. As part of their journey to seek new expression of church, and to heed Jesus' command to "Love your neighbors", they started to explore ways to bring "church" to their neighborhood. They took off their corporate hats and started 73@Hillcrest, a missional bistro just up the street from their home. They not only served amazing food and great beer but also became a gathering point where neighbors met to share life and to find hope. The hours were long, and the work was hard, but Yau Boon and Cheryl engaged in kingdom mission outside the walls of the cathedral, bringing the love of Jesus right where their neighbors are. They embraced a bring "church to people" lifestyle, instead of "come-to-my church" mindset, inviting kingdom minded folks to their bistro to share their missional stories and experiences with their community. Jim Yost who frequently speaks in prominent churches in Singapore and other nations once came to 73@Hillcrest and shared of his preference for this setting than the big congregation where he had spoken that morning.

In summary, living the Gospel's values in love and practical impact attracts and transforms communities. This in contrast to the mindset displayed in the United States by Evangelicals which assumes a central moral role in the community and expects everyone to abide by the outward acceptance of its rules and regulations for life.

My experiences have confirmed that, the Gospel of Jesus message is clear: embracing community as it is and displaying service-oriented faith will change lives.

CANCER

Four years after my return to California, I was in Germany for the annual Freakstock festival, sponsored by Jesus Freaks International. On an early morning walk, I received a call from my youngest brother, Art. His voice was thick with the weight of addiction, and I tried to console him, unaware of his worsening health. A few days later, he was gone, taken by an undetected stomach cancer at 52. Art was an artist in his own right, recognized in 2012 as the best flooring contractor in Colorado Springs. From his childhood days in Venezuela caring for his chickens, to his musical talents playing the organ and flute, he had a vibrant spirit. However, after moving to the USA during his high school years, he faced struggles, getting involved with gangs and falling into drug use. His bond with my son Zak was special, acting as his protector. His passing deeply affected our family, reminding me of our father's own battle with cancer in 1990.

By fall 2018, my elevated PSA levels suggested prostate cancer. Before heading to Taiwan for a family wedding, I consulted a specialist at UCSF. The suggested treatments involved surgery and chemotherapy, which I wasn't keen on. Through research, I learned of an innovative treatment from Israel, which used targeted lasers to eradicate cancer cells. Dr. Sperling in Florida offered this, and after ensuring I met their criteria, I was off to Miami, where my brother Willie, from Colorado, was waiting.

The procedure was straightforward, and subsequent tests showed a marked improvement. The entire journey, from diagnosis to treatment, was a testament to my faith and trust in both medical advancements and a higher power.

This experience brought memories flooding back from 34 years ago when I accompanied my father to his doctor. I was the interpreter of his grim diagnosis, a role I'll never forget. My father's unwavering faith in God was admirable. That faith saw him through six challenging years before he passed away peacefully.

Now, as I faced my own health challenges, my father's faith echoed in my decisions and actions. After the successful procedure, I was soon back to Taiwan, alongside Vivien, celebrating the union of her second son Andrew to Shirlene.

In 2022, I faced a challenging recurrence: my prostate cancer returned. At that point, my initial thought was to approach Dr. Sperling, who recommended a relatively new but promising treatment known as HIFU (High Intensity Focused Ultrasound). This technique was emerging as a powerful tool against prostate cancer, and Dr. Sperling was among the specialists administering it.

However, during a vacation in the picturesque coastal town of Puerto Vallarta, Mexico, I stumbled upon an alternative. It was there that I first heard of Dr. Carlos Garcia of UroVallarta, a prominent urologist with a sterling reputation. Intrigued, I reached out to him, and what I found was a pleasant surprise: he offered the exact same HIFU procedure, but for a fraction of the price I would have paid in the USA.

Recognizing the potential, my wife Vivien and I decided to embark on this medical journey. We took a three-hour flight to meet Dr. Garcia. From our first interaction, I was struck by his unmatched professionalism and the genuine care he exhibited. It was unparalleled and beyond anything I had experienced with medical professionals back in the USA. He even went the extra mile, giving me his personal contact number and ensuring I could reach out to him anytime.

A year post-procedure, the results spoke for themselves. My PSA levels, which are a key indicator of prostate cancer, had dropped significantly. This was a testament to the effectiveness of the HIFU treatment. However, the recovery journey wasn't without its challenges. Various health issues arose, but with each hurdle, Dr. Garcia was right there, offering his unwavering support and guidance.

Beyond his clinic, Dr. Garcia's dedication to his profession and to innovation was evident. He took it upon himself to expand the reach of this life-saving technique. He recently undertook a trip to China, where he conducted training sessions for local doctors in various cities, ensuring that they were well-equipped to administer the HIFU procedure.

Throughout my life, I've encountered numerous situations where I felt the shadow of danger. These moments, though perilous, allowed me to connect deeper with my faith. I recall the harrowing experience in El Salvador, where I and a group of fellow Americans were stopped by armed guerrillas. As the only Latino among us, I found myself thrust into the role of the group's spokesperson. The weight of the situation gave me a newfound courage, and I managed to negotiate our safety.

Furthermore, my travels led to multiple detentions by border authorities in cities from Tel Aviv to London. Particularly challenging was an incident in London where confidential letters were found on my person. The letters, entrusted to me by Ghais Malik, the Anglican Bishop in Egypt from 1985 to 2000, were meant for the Archbishop of Canterbury, detailing the plight of Muslim converts in Cairo.

There were also moments of sheer terror: a plane engine failure above India and a turbulent ferry ride across the English Channel amidst a raging storm. These instances, combined with my ongoing health battle, solidified my belief in divine intervention. I began to recognize these as "Jesus Moments." They were profound experiences that highlighted the unshakeable nature of the faith I held dear. They were moments of spiritual clarity, where the teachings and assurances of Jesus became tangibly real, especially in circumstances where I felt overwhelmed.

At the core of my beliefs is the essence of the Gospel. It speaks of life in its truest, most untainted form. Jesus's mission was to restore Creation to its pristine state, aiming to heal life's inherent brokenness and sorrow. This profound engagement with the Gospel is transformative. Once you've experienced its depth, it leaves an indelible mark on your soul, forever changing your perspective on life.

HISTORICAL AND
CULTURAL REFLECTIONS

VENEZUELA: NAVIGATING THROUGH THE ECHOES OF HISTORY

From 1999, with Hugo Chavez's ascendancy to power, to his demise in 2013, Venezuela underwent a troubled transformation. With an oil-rich economy boosting the nation's coffers, Venezuelans initially basked in improved access to essential amenities like food, shelter, healthcare, and education. However, the nation's underlying structural corruption went unaddressed, rendering these reforms fleeting. Nicolas Maduro, Chavez's mentee, succeeded him. The Wall Street Journal once acknowledged Maduro, a former bus driver and trade union leader, as "the Chavez circle's most adept administrator and politician." Nevertheless, by his second year in office, the nation faced escalating shortages and plummeting living standards. This provoked widespread protests, met with stringent state clampdowns. By 2019, The New York Times pointedly attributed Venezuela's plunging economic state and humanitarian crisis to Maduro's egregious mismanagement.

It was heartbreaking to witness, more so because most of my family resided in Venezuela. They soon became part of a staggering exodus - 7 million, or 21% of the population, according to the UNHCR. These citizens sought refuge from the escalating violence, threats, and the alarming scarcity of fundamental resources.

For more than half a century, I hadn't met a single Venezuelan immigrant. Yet, post-crisis, I encountered several, even within my own family, now dispersed from the U.S. to Paris and Sydney. Most had taken arduous journeys on foot across Colombia or Brazil's borders.

From 2016, my concerns gravitated towards those left behind. One person who stood out was Abihail Lara, my then 30-year-old cousin and pastor at a Baptist Church. Our daily interactions revolved around the spiraling challenges his community faced. Traditional evangelical teachings offered little consolation. So, together, we sought divine insights for modern-day chaotic Venezuela.

This led Abihail to rethink theological pedagogy, birthing the Hagios Online Institute in 2016 (Hagios means "Holy" in Greek). The institution aimed at nurturing leader's adept in biblical tenets and hands-on skills to alleviate local issues. By 2023, they held their first graduation in Cabimas, western Venezuela.

Simultaneously, my wife, Vivien, felt a divine urge to invest in Venezuelan agriculture. Coincidentally, this aligned with Abihail's and my discussions. Consequently, Abihail acquired land in Colonia Tovar, a quaint town west of the capital city Caracas. This region, with its rich history of German immigrants and fertile terrain, offered an opportunity to purchase land parcels. Abihail and his youthful team embraced agricultural endeavors, embodying the ethos that would underpin Hagios's curriculum. Drawing inspiration from biblical parables and employing sustainable agricultural practices, they witnessed three prosperous harvests annually.

However, with economic despair, Venezuela saw an alarming spike in suicides. An independent watchdog estimated that Caracas, in 2017, registered almost as many suicides as the entire nation had in 2012. To combat this, we adapted Zimbabwe's Friendship Bench program, successfully run by trained grandmothers. Renamed "Amigos a la Mano" in Venezuela, it garnered substantial support from mental health professionals and religious institutions.

Furthermore, as the COVID pandemic unfolded, Abihail's team turned adversities into opportunities. They began producing affordable triple-layered face masks. They also launched a graphic design service catering to budding entrepreneurs.

With the pandemic's gradual decline and the dollar's adoption stabilizing the economy, Venezuela began showing signs of recovery. Some even began to repatriate. Seizing this opportunity, we acquired a facility in Valencia. Today, it serves as our nerve center, supporting new enterprises, our mental health initiatives, educational endeavors through Hagios, and facilitating direct sale of our agricultural produce at better prices.

In essence, Venezuela's story is a testament to its indomitable spirit, proving that even in the darkest hours, hope and innovation can pave the way to recovery.

LIVING OUR CONVICTIONS

Throughout the various shifts and developments in Venezuela, I've come to see how my association with Next Step has evolved, transforming full circle. I left the heart of Venezuela when I was a mere 17, dedicating myself to causes and services around the globe, except ironically in my birthplace. Now, standing at the age of 65, I see with clarity a vibrant new generation rising, eagerly taking on leadership roles. Through my experiences and observations, I've come to a profound understanding that in the realm of Kingdom leadership, the true essence of authority resides solely with the Lord. Whatever authority we think we possess is merely a trust, a delegation, and should be approached with utmost humility. This significant insight became clear to me during the pivotal 1987 event in Singapore, specifically designed as an international gathering for budding evangelical leaders.

However, a striking disparity I've noticed is that many leaders around me, instead of embracing this humble mindset, adhered strongly to a patriarchal one. They held a firm belief, implying that their divine call was superior, making them more adept than others. I count myself fortunate to have internalized a vital lesson early on: while the Lord may have chosen me for a particular purpose, He has equally chosen countless others. Moreover, in our rapidly advancing world, with its unique challenges, it's crucial for both men and women from this generation to rise and prove their mettle. It beckons the question, who among us is prepared to gracefully pass on the leadership baton to the next?

Seeking insight and perspective on this matter, I've extended an invitation to Abihail, also hailing from Venezuela, to share his narrative on how I'm passing the baton to him in the succeeding chapter.

A NEW DIRECTION

KINGDOM MYSTERIES AND OUR FAMILY LINKS BY ABIHAIL LARA

Wolfgang is a citizen of the world; yet he carries his native country with him. Although, it is true that his life and his ministry have gone in many directions, far from Venezuela, even so, his land has always been present in his heart and mind. This is evident, since, even at a distance, he has been able to inspire actions that are blessing to his people.

This chapter is a narrative of how God has fulfilled His promise to our family and how in His goodness, has united both of us by invisible threads throughout history, so that today, we can see how the Kingdom spreads stealthily in every corner of society and how our lives take on meaning in the light of a much broader framework that tells the story of the reconciliation of all things in Christ. I thank the author for allowing me to give witness to what God has done in our lives, ministries, and our nation.

From my earliest memories, I was always enveloped in the comforting and guiding influence of the gospel within my family. During my formative years, I frequented a Baptist church, which was the brainchild of my revered Uncle Daniel, Wolfgang father. He was more than just a family member; he was an emblem, a beacon of devotion to the gospel's teachings, whose writings and photographic memories continue to inspire countless like me.

His unwavering commitment led him to preach the gospel's message in a quaint Venezuelan hamlet. Subsequently, a significant portion of our extended family made a collective decision to relocate from the bustling city of Caracas to this serene location. They laid the foundation of a humble Bible study group there. As word spread and the group flourished, they formed an alliance with a prominent Baptist church in Caracas. This collaboration aimed at nurturing this nascent mission, culminating in the establishment of a church on a piece of land generously donated by a family member.

During this familial migratory wave, my own parents, along with my siblings and I, became part of this blossoming community. It was in this nurturing environment that I was first introduced to the enlightening world of the gospel. Following Uncle Daniel's departure, the once close-knit community experienced fragmentation.

A significant turning point in my life was my return to the church at the age of 16. This was facilitated by my joining a basketball team, spearheaded by a dynamic pastor. This team, with its mix of devout believers and youth like me, was an evangelistic initiative. It was here that I wholeheartedly embraced my faith and swiftly discerned my life's calling. Recognizing my genuine zeal, Grandma Lourdes, fondly called "Malule" by all, bestowed upon me a cherished heirloom: a Bible dictionary previously owned by Uncle Daniel. This gesture felt like the symbolic passing of the family ministerial mantel. An elder pastor, close witness of my journey, once remarked, "In you, God ensures your family legacy continues, always anointing a prophet."

This antique dictionary served as a guiding star in my rigorous Bible studies, kindling an unmatched passion within me. Recognizing my potential, a kind-hearted individual anonymously sponsored my education at a regional Bible institute. A mere two years later, I found myself at the Baptist Theological Seminary of Venezuela, embarking on comprehensive theological studies.

So, you might be wondering why I'm going into so much detail about my life, right? Well, there's a pretty cool connection here. You see, the dictionary was a gift Wolfgang gave to his Dad, my Uncle Daniel back in 1986, just over a year before I was born. When Uncle Daniel passed, the dictionary was given to our Grandma Malule as an heirloom of her first son. When our Grandma gifts me this book, she symbolically brings Wolfgang and my life together 12 years before we ever even talked. It's like a torch being passed down from Wolfgang to his Dad and then to Grandma and now to me, Abihail Lara. This torch is like a symbol that ties together three generations of gospel ministers: Uncle Daniel from the past, Wolfgang in the present, and me, hopefully carrying hope for our future.

THE FIRST STEPS INTO THE KINGDOM

By 2016, Venezuela's political, social, and economic climate reached a critical juncture. Numerous pastors left the country, leaving churches in a dire state. The massive recession impacted every Venezuelan. Finding essential food or hygiene products meant enduring long lines, and even then, there was no guarantee of securing supplies. In this bleak setting, Wolfgang, who I knew distantly, grew increasingly concerned about Venezuela. He reached out to me, curious about the general situation, our ministry, and everyday life.

During this period, I was leading a burgeoning church and pursuing a master's degree at the same seminary where I'd completed my undergraduate studies. To make ends meet, I ran a modest carpentry shop in La Colonia Tovar—a town established by German immigrants, which now thrived on agriculture and tourism. This backdrop fostered shared aspirations and projects between Wolfgang and me. Wolfgang envisioned a strategy to address the nation's challenges, leading to the purchase of four hectares of land. We began cultivating this land, not only to create job opportunities but also to produce food. Concurrently, I suggested establishing a holistic Christian leadership training institute, leveraging online education to guide the new pastors stepping up due to the exodus from Venezuela.

As our trust grew, we initiated a farming enterprise. Even during Venezuela's darkest hours, our efforts bore fruit—literally and metaphorically—as we provided sustenance to churches and organizations aiding the needy. Simultaneously, we laid the groundwork for the Hagios Comprehensive Training Institute, which has since trained over a hundred dedicated individuals in diverse programs. These programs fuse robust theological foundations with hands-on components that foster impactful ministry actions.

A TRANSFORMATIVE BOND

Partnering with Wolfgang has been enlightening. He is dedicated to mentoring individuals, ensuring they create a global ripple effect, and I'm honored to be one of his mentees. He believes in empowering others to further the Kingdom, a principle that's reshaped my perception and approach to ministry.

While I've always been rooted in the Baptist church and hold my convictions dearly, my journey with Wolfgang has broadened my understanding of the Kingdom of God. I've come to realize that it transcends mere doctrines and principles—it's an ever-present force in every societal aspect. We see ourselves as ambassadors, embedding every solution with God's purpose of redemption through Christ. This revelation has expanded our horizons, allowing us to bring about changes with a gospel that's dynamic and reliant on God's action within and through us.

This fresh perspective has fortified my belief that my ministerial role isn't confined to ecclesiastical dynamics. Instead, it encompasses a holistic view of God's redemptive plan in every facet of life—a vision we're wholly dedicated to.

Despite Venezuela's ongoing challenges, our resolve remains unshaken. We've also established Next Step in Venezuela, rallying others towards a vision of the Kingdom that rejuvenates both church and societal frameworks. Currently, Next Step Venezuela comprises over twenty members, all working on diverse projects from education and entrepreneurship to church planting and media.

A MEMORABLE ENCOUNTER

Our connection through friendship, shared ministry, and continuous learning has been a remarkable journey that has spanned nearly seven years. What makes this connection even more intriguing is that Wolfgang and I didn't meet in person until the year 2019. Until then, our interactions had primarily been through the digital realm, yet the bond we had formed was already strong.

In 2019, a pivotal moment arrived when Wolfgang and his wife, Vivien, embarked on a journey to Bogotá. My wife, Belkys, and I did the same, bridging the physical distance that had separated us for so long. The meeting was a significant milestone in our relationship and cemented our deep camaraderie dedicated to the service of God's Kingdom.

During our time together in Bogotá, we not only explored the city but also had the opportunity to connect with partners from various organizations who shared our passion for ministry and service. It was a time of fruitful collaboration and brainstorming, as we sought fresh avenues to contribute to our shared mission.

One of the most impactful aspects of that meeting was getting to know Vivien on a deeper level. Her unwavering commitment to her faith and her incredible generosity towards the Kingdom of God left a lasting impression on me. As a successful businesswoman, she exemplifies the idea that business can be a powerful tool in the service of the Kingdom, challenging the misconception that it's solely about profit.

Wolfgang and Vivien have continued to serve as pillars of inspiration in my life. Our encounter in Bogotá ignited a renewed sense of purpose and dedication within me. It was a reminder of the trust and faith they had bestowed upon us, which only fueled our determination to serve, innovate, and make a meaningful impact in our respective ministries.

In the years since that memorable meeting, our connection has grown stronger, and our collaboration has continued to bear fruit. The lessons learned from Wolfgang and Vivien continue to guide our path, reminding us of the incredible potential that lies in a shared commitment to serving God's Kingdom.

NEW OPPORTUNITIES AND NEW CHALLENGES

"Next Step Venezuela" www.nextstepvzla.com represents the series of initiatives we've launched in the nation. Currently, our efforts are centered in Valencia, located in Carabobo State. This city, once flourishing due to its vast industrial and commercial capacities, holds significant business potential. In 2021, we expanded our presence to Valencia, acquiring and renovating a modest building. This became a self-sufficient operational hub, not only serving as the academic venue for the Hagios Comprehensive Training Institute but also fostering new endeavors. We implemented a business model ensuring the site's longevity, introducing a coworking space. Numerous entrepreneurs utilize this space to bolster their ventures, either through teaching or operating directly from the location.

We were also fortunate to receive a donation of radio transmission equipment from a supportive church. This prompted us to venture into the media sector, setting up a radio station aligned with contemporary communication styles. Every initiative we undertake adheres to three core principles: (1) Bear witness to the Kingdom of God, (2) Foster opportunities to empower others in their ministry, and (3) Generate employment while promoting sustainable endeavors. These tenets guide each project and shape our approach to every new opportunity.

In La Colonia Tovar, we persist in our agricultural endeavors, planting both commercially viable and cost-effective crops. This initiative serves the dual purpose of supporting our team and the broader community. Managed by a group of local young farmers, we're launching fresh efforts on the land, aiming for community enhancement, kingdom values, and inclusive opportunities. Moreover, we've set up a small garment production unit. As the municipality's pioneer textile manufacturer, we produce school uniforms and casual wear, employing five dedicated individuals.

Of note is our commitment to mentorship. In both the agricultural initiatives in La Colonia and communication efforts in Valencia, we involve talented young individuals. Drawing from the guidance I received from Wolfgang, I now mentor them, assisting in every project phase. Our vision remains unwavering. Alongside Fabiana (my 3-year-old daughter), Belkys (my wife), and a growing team, we aspire for a Venezuela where the Kingdom of God is palpable. Our aim is to inspire communities of faith to be agents of comprehensive transformation in their surroundings.

NEW CONVICTIONS

During Donald Trump's era, the societal fabric of America experienced profound shifts, which brought significant concerns regarding the alignment of modern practices with the teachings of the Gospel. Acts 4:47 indicates that early Christians were distinguished by their love and compassion. However, during this period, I saw a rising tide of intolerance and exclusion all supported by the majority of American Evangelicals.

There's the perception that the United States is a place where anyone can make it, is now at a crucial juncture, reevaluating its identity. Historically, the voices of dissent against America came from abroad. Palestinians in Gaza grieved for their lost ones, Mullahs in Tehran expressed their animosity, and opposition came from leaders in countries like Cuba and Venezuela. Yet, what's distinct about the current situation is that the most poignant critiques are internal. This inward reflection is reminiscent of the tumultuous period following the assassination of Martin Luther King Jr.

The nation has seen its share of tragedies. The Newtown, CT massacre of 2017 stands as a grim reminder, being the deadliest elementary school shooting. Not far behind was the Las Vegas incident that resulted in the loss of 60 innocent lives. And places like Buffalo and Uvalde became synonymous with the grave problem of gun violence that's plaguing the country. The data for 2020, as provided by the CDC, recorded 45,222 firearm-related fatalities, marking an alarming 13.5% rise from the previous year. What's even more shocking is the fact that gun-related deaths have now become the leading cause of death among the younger population.

To grasp the enormity of this issue, one can look to historical and religious texts. The story of Cain and Abel in the book of Genesis is instructive. Driven by jealousy, Cain took the life of his brother, prompting God to proclaim that the blood of the slain cries out from the earth. The books of Psalms and Proverbs carry warnings about the repercussions of shedding innocent blood. The New Testament, especially in the book of Matthew, portrays Jesus as the embodiment of non-violence. He warned that those who take up the sword shall also perish by it.

However, despite the overwhelming evidence pointing to a gun violence crisis, attempts to impose stricter firearm regulations in the U.S. often meet resistance. The Second Amendment is frequently cited as the primary reason for this reluctance. For many Americans and Evangelicals in particular, the U.S. Constitution is the bedrock on which their beliefs are built, even more than the Bible. This isn't inherently problematic because the Constitution seeks to guarantee rights for all citizens, irrespective of their religious affiliations. The issue arises when individuals begin to view these constitutional rights as "God-given," a conviction held by some who don't even subscribe to Biblical tenets.

The opening lines of the U.S. Constitution emphasize "Life, Liberty, and the pursuit of Happiness." The Bill of Rights further amplifies this by providing the right to bear arms. The framers believed in the intrinsic right to self-defense. However, while this idea is integral to the American spirit, it doesn't always mesh with Biblical teachings.

Representative Matt Schaefer of Texas, following the West Texas shooting, took to Twitter to express his views. He was adamant about not letting the misdeeds of a few take away the "God-given rights" of the many. Senator Ted Cruz, a regular presence at NRA conventions, echoed similar sentiments. Instead of pointing fingers at firearms, Cruz emphasized addressing the deeper cultural and societal issues that lead to such violent outbursts. Both Cruz and Donald Trump have championed the belief that a well-armed citizenry can act as a deterrent to potential threats.

While there's some merit to this argument, and it aligns with the foundational principles of America, one cannot equate every aspect of the country's gun laws with divine endorsement. The mingling of Constitutional rights with divine proclamations muddies the waters when it comes to formulating solutions to complex societal challenges.

To navigate the troubled waters of gun violence, it's essential to differentiate between rights granted by the Constitution and teachings from religious texts. Beyond this, a broader approach is needed, addressing mental health, societal norms, and other underlying causes of this violence. The road ahead demands collaboration, understanding, and a recognition of the multifaceted nature of the problem.

In summation, while both the Bible and the Constitution offer valuable insights, the real test lies in interpreting and applying their teachings in today's context. Only by harmoniously merging these principles can America hope to stem the tide of violence and lay the foundation for a safer, more harmonious future for all its residents.

As an outgrowth of American identity, when some Christians assert that the Constitution and the Bible converge to make gun ownership a "God-given right," they inadvertently unveil a faith that intertwines more with patriotism than Jesus's teachings. This dissonance was palpable in the electoral support for Donald Trump and lawmakers merging national symbols with religious texts.

One revelation during the Trump tenure was America's painful reality in our persistent racial scars. Popular narratives trace America's history to the Mayflower's 1620 arrival. Yet, in 1619, John Rolfe, an English settler known for tobacco cultivation in Virginia and his union with Pocahontas, informed Sir Edwin Sandy about "20 and odd negroes" — enslaved Africans delivered by a Dutch ship. They likely initiated the gruesome saga of African enslavement that lasted until the 14th Amendment of 1868 recognized their voting rights and birthright citizenship.

However, the specter of the Jim Crow era, with its racial segregation, still haunts African Americans. The 1965 Voting Rights Act aimed at rectification, but 2013

Supreme Court verdict relaxed voting restrictions in certain states and most recently attempts to restrict voter registration are still being disputed in courts.

This history was crystallized for me by the Black Lives Matter (BLM) movement, born after distressing events like the murders of Trayvon Martin and George Floyd. The movement's 2020 global resonance was staggering, with up to 26 million protesters. A 2020 Pew poll found 67% of American adults supporting BLM.

Participating in our own two BLM marches in Millbrae, where Asians are 49% of residents, I learned about Chinedu Okobi's 2018 murder after an altercation down the street from our house with a Sheriff deputy.

TWO BECOMING ONE

Vivien and I will celebrate our 15-year marriage anniversary in 2024. Our journey has had its fair share of ups and downs. Thanks to God's boundless grace, our love for each other remains strong. We cherish our daily walks in the neighborhood, hand in hand. Our culinary preferences differ; she isn't fond of some foods I relish, and I fail to understand her penchant for nocturnal ocean swims. Nevertheless, our hearts and minds grow increasingly unified.

As we both approach 65 (she's six months my senior), I reflect on a statement I made five years prior, about shifting our work focus by our 65th birthdays. I'm not contemplating traditional retirement. Instead, I aspire to guide others in realizing their callings. Our vision encompasses our eight children, five (soon seven!) grandchildren, and extends to many others. I'm currently mentoring two Venezuelans. Jose, our neighbor, manages our vacation rentals and works as an Uber driver. Abihail, based in Venezuela, pioneers innovative mission enterprises. Our circle also includes Hengky in Jakarta, Philemon in Athens, Shannon in London, Kate in Shanghai and Florian in Taunusstein, Germany to name a few.

My heart yearns to collaborate with Vivien in serving our local and global community. We aim to ignite the passions of those we mentor. Abihail has been instrumental in imparting invaluable insights. His attributes include hard work, entrepreneurial acumen, theological dedication, and the ability to align creative solutions with Biblical principles. In May 2019, unable to visit Venezuela, we met Abihail and his wife, Belkis, in Bogota, Colombia. Despite our first face-to-face encounter, our rapport was instantaneous. We deliberated on introducing Next Step to Venezuela, a nation grappling with challenges yet unwavering in hope. We foresee innovative mission practices that will further God's Kingdom.

The Gospel's essence is unity. When individuals harness their gifts collaboratively, the perceived divide between the secular and sacred diminishes. People lead lives that bless those around them both spiritually and mentally, drawing them nearer to God and the community.

In the 90s, a German prophet predicted that divine solutions to life's complex problems would be revealed to those who solely attribute their success to God.

The Bible frequently touches on God unveiling hidden truths. For instance, Luke 8:17-18 speaks of revelations, and Luke 10:21 celebrates the divine wisdom granted to the innocent. Additionally, scriptures in Ezekiel 47:12 and Revelation 22:2-3 depict the curative powers of trees' fruits and leaves.

We've witnessed this revelation firsthand through Hogan Bassey, co-founder of LivFul with Matt Elsberry. LivFul, a health and community development enterprise, seeks to unlock human potential. Akiva™, their flagship product, is an insect repellent developed to provide lasting protection against insect-borne diseases. It's gaining regulatory approvals in countries like Australia, New Zealand, Singapore, the USA, the Philippines, and China.

Dr. Ronald Ross's 1897 discovery that mosquitoes transmit malaria revolutionized preventive measures. Yet, mosquitoes remain lethal, causing over a million deaths annually. A recent NY Times report highlighted a resilient new mosquito species causing concern. Following this, Akiva was introduced to the Nigerian market.

LivFul has provided Vivien and me a collaborative platform. Vivien was among the early investors, and I've played a role in aligning the product with religious organizations. As LivFul garners attention from investors and experts, it's poised to spearhead life science advancements. We're eager to introduce Akiva, the insect repellent to countries like Venezuela, which has seen a resurgence of mosquito-borne diseases. The fight continues.

CONCLUSION

CONCLUSION: RECOVERING THE GOSPEL

How do we truly live out the Gospel recapturing its essence in this 21st century? The simple response is by embracing real community with individuals who recognize their shared need for a central force, drawing them closer to one another. For us, this force is the teachings of the Lord Jesus, especially His commandment to love God and our neighbors as we love ourselves, as found in Matthew 22:36-40. There's no need for songs, preaching, ceremonies, budgets, salaries, or programs. The primary requirement is the willingness to engage in genuine relationships. Everything else unfolds organically, guided by the Spirit.

At our very essence, Vivien and I thrive on connecting with new individuals, inviting them to dine with us at our table, and eventually sharing our lives with them. I firmly believe that hospitality is the most essential quality for anyone hoping to unite people.

But how can you tell if hospitality runs deep within you? We were all designed for relationships. The straightforward answer is that your home doesn't need to be pristine to welcome guests. Our unwavering faith in Jesus and His teachings empowers and equips us to first cater to our needs and then to those of others.

An example of this type of group is our spiritual community which began with Tim Halls, residing 31 miles from my home, just across the San Francisco Bay. I then introduced two other friends into our tight-knit group, expanding our connections even further geographically. As time progressed, our group grew with the addition of more friends, some invited by the initial members. Five years ago, we began convening weekly to uplift and support one another, a testament to our cohesive bond.

Tim and I initially met in 1981, both serving in OC Ministries, a missionary organization that later evolved into Dawn Ministries. Currently semi-retired,

Tim sought companions to share the highs and lows of the second half of life. His extensive service in Latin America afforded him an intimate understanding of my cultural roots. We both were open about our challenges, commonly concealed by those in the ministry, fostering mutual respect and understanding. Our shared fondness for German cuisine and IPA beer, especially on his side of the Bay, further solidified our bond.

In 2016, Vivien and I received Andrew Jones and his children. Andrew was battling the effects of malaria contracted in West Africa and grieving the loss of his beloved wife, Debbie, our dear friend, to the same disease. Debbie's fresh perspectives on simplicity and raw authenticity greatly influenced us. Andrew, alongside Debbie since 2000, made me cognizant of the marginalized youth, and he assisted me in diverse ways, from setting up websites to plumbing tasks for our vacation rental business in Pacifica.

Andrew, typically reserved, initially joined my sessions with Tim for intellectual debate. However, over time, he shared the emotional void left by Debbie's demise and how it affected his ability to stay focused.

Before returning from Beijing in 2012, I encountered Dave Nothhelfer at a San Francisco gathering. He was acquainted with many from our overseas community. Our shared passion for missions, the environment, and the underprivileged established a firm connection. A marine biologist, Dave enlightened me on the Christian responsibility to protect God's creations. Living alone in Oakland, it was convenient to spend time with him. Our trust deepened as Dave shared his tumultuous past and yearning for familial warmth. After returning from The Philippines, Dave came to live in our home as part of our family.

Eventually, Tim, Andrew, Dave and I began meeting, reaping the mutual benefits of investing in each other's lives. Our gatherings diversified beyond the German restaurant, discussing life, missions, and theology, always making time to pray for one another.

We all actively participated in our local churches, engaging in various groups and events. However, within our small group of four, we discovered a profound bond, mutual understanding, and trust we had yearned for. This intimate connection is pivotal in truly embracing the Gospel and is best nurtured within a small circle, where everyone can genuinely listen and express themselves. This setting fosters trust and care, enabling individuals to dispel inherent biases and judgmental tendencies. We witnessed the Gospel's transformative power, allowing authentic love to dissolve our fears, forging genuine community bonds.

While each of us was wrapped up in our personal lives and commitments, our fellowship had a unique quality to it. For instance, Tim is a proud father of three daughters, two of whom are married with children of their own. Andrew, originally from New Zealand, has five children residing everywhere from the U.S. East Coast to New Zealand. Two of my children live a stone's throw away, while the rest are scattered nationwide. Our family lives contrast sharply with the deliberate unity of our fellowship, presenting individual challenges and growth opportunities.

As racial tensions intensified in the U.S., particularly after the tragic murder of George Floyd, our group began engaging in profound conversations about racism's implications in our lives and the Gospel's stance on it. Eager for diverse perspectives, we welcomed Roy Garanton, a Venezuelan finishing his doctorate in International and Multicultural Education with a focus on Race and Justice. Roy shared his first-hand experiences with prejudice when he came with his parents who served as Venezuelan missionaries to Oklahoma.

We were also joined by William Hay, a Hong Kong-based attorney with Mayflower ancestry. Our bond with William first grew from shared interests in the Gospel's social implications.

The onset of the COVID-19 pandemic restructured our meetings. The shift to virtual gatherings allowed distant members, like William, to participate from Hong Kong. We expanded our circle, including David Kludt, a local pastor originally from Wisconsin now involved in film making. Dr. Clarence Schuler, a prominent Black leader. Clarence then introduced us to Jerry Kelow and Jerry King.

One might wonder, what binds such a diverse group? The answer is Christ. He is our universal savior and the core of our existence. He exemplifies the ideal life, guiding us in our pursuit of righteousness.

We convene every Monday at 4:30 PST, updating one another on our lives, praying, and grappling with the Gospel's contemporary relevance.

Our desire for humility in all interactions has burgeoned. We've grown to cherish the edict of loving our neighbors and even perceiving adversaries as kin. Although our viewpoints don't always converge, we've learned the art of listening, agreeing to disagree, and holding our beliefs with open hands.

Our assembly is now our spiritual family. We intercede and assist each other, even financially. Within this milieu, I've gleaned a renewed comprehension of the Gospel, pushing me to chronicle the gaps I observe among Evangelicals.

Roy encouraged us to amplify our inclusivity. We welcome more female voices and those from the LGBTQ+ community. We've embraced this counsel, actively striving to understand and assimilate the diverse voices God uses to mold us, manifesting His celestial kingdom on earth.

Recently, our discussions have revolved around the topic of Reparations, aiming to align our perspectives with the Gospel's teachings.

I believe that such groups, accommodating both believers and skeptics, held together by mutual respect and frequent interactions, can rejuvenate the Gospel in people's hearts. I challenge you my dear reader to foster such connections, listening intently to both peers and the divine. Recently, a local friend proposed purchasing a building for community service and prayer. In response, I suggested a more grassroots approach: a house in every street serving as a center for spiritual reflection. Embracing the reality that the Kingdom of God resides within us can set the stage for profound change.

www.ingramcontent.com/pod-product-compliance
Lightning Source LLC
Chambersburg PA
CBHW031429120626
46545CB00006B/2330